Maximum Solutions for ADD, Learning Disabilities and Autism

Maximum Solutions for ADD, Learning Disabilities and Autism

Ted Broer

SILOAM PRESS

Living in Health—Body, Mind and Spirit

MAXIMUM SOLUTIONS FOR ADD, LEARNING DISABILITIES AND AUTISM
by Ted Broer
Published by Siloam Press
A part of Strang Communications Company
600 Rinehart Road
Lake Mary, Florida 32746
www.siloampress.com

Unless otherwise noted, all Scripture quotations are from the Holy Bible, the New King James Version. Copyright © 1979, 1980, 1982 by Thomas Nelson, Inc., publishers. Used by permission.

Scripture quotations marked NLT are from the Holy Bible, New Living Translation. Copyright © 1996. Used by permission of Tyndale House Publishers, Inc., Wheaton, IL 60189. All rights reserved.

Cover design by Judith McKittrick

Library of Congress Catalog Card Number: 2001096730
International Standard Book Number: 0-88419-719-0

This book is not intended to provide medical advice or to take the place of medical advice and treatment from your personal physician. Readers are advised to consult their own doctors or other qualified health professionals regarding the treatment of their medical problems. Neither the publisher nor the author takes any responsibility for any possible consequences from any treatment, action or application of medicine, supplement, herb or preparation to any person reading or following the information in this book. If readers are taking prescription medications, they should consult with their physicians and not take themselves off of medicines to start supplementation without the proper supervision of a physician.

02 03 04 05 06   9 8 7 6 5 4 3 2 1
Printed in the United States of America

DEDICATION

This book is dedicated to all of the wonderful, hardworking and loving parents who have struggled with ADD, ADHD and autism. I hope and pray that you are able to use this information to help your loved ones and those with whom you come in contact. If you have any questions, please do not hesitate to contact me.

ACKNOWLEDGMENTS

A special thanks to talk show host Marlin Maddoux for always speaking the truth about controversial issues. He and his staff are a credit to their profession.

Contents

10 Reversing the Dietary Devastation of the Television Generation 139

INTRODUCTION

Reaping a Bitter Harvest

D rugging school children has become a multimillion-dollar business in the United States. In 1998, the U.S. National Institute of Mental Health (NIMH) predicted that ten million American school children would be taking psychiatric drugs for one reason or another by the year 2000![1] Although the NIMH hasn't confirmed whether or not this gloomy prediction came true, a research report in the *Journal of the American Medical Association* said that prescriptions of stimulants to two- to four-year-olds has increased 300 percent![2]

What is happening to our children? Did you know there are approximately five to seven million children in the United States diagnosed with ADD? As early as 1995, the International Narcotics Control Board (INCB) of the World Health Organization issued a public statement that said, "Ten to 12 percent of all boys between the ages of six and fourteen in the United States have been diagnosed as having ADD and are being treated with methylphenidate [Ritalin]."

Evidently, medical experts in other nations noticed long ago what the American medical establishment refused to see or acknowledge. Two years later, the same narcotics board said, "The therapeutic use of methylphenidate is now under scrutiny by the American medical community; the INCB welcomes this."[3]

Sadly, it appears that all they did was look at the problem, but never acted. The big business of drugging school children is booming as never before! In November 1999, the U.S. Drug Enforcement Administration (DEA) issued an alarming statistic that confirmed from the "supply side" of the equation what the World Health Organization had warned us about: There was a six-fold increase in Ritalin production between 1990 and 1995, and America is the biggest user—pardon me for my lack of political correctness—the biggest consumer of Ritalin in the world. We use or "consume" approximately 90 percent of the world's Ritalin![4] (And most of it went into our kids.) Our country is using a great deal of this incredibly dangerous drug, and a lot of drug companies are making a lot of money.

HAVE YOU TAKEN YOUR PSYCHOTROPIC DRUG, DEAR?

Millions of American children start their day with prescription drugs that are so powerful and dangerous that they are banned from the streets by federal drug and narcotics agencies.[5]

Dr. Peter R. Breggin, a psychiatrist and director of the International Center for the Study of Psychiatry and Psychology, testified before a congressional subcommittee, "With 53 million children enrolled in school, probably more than five million are taking stimulant drugs."[6] That means that nearly one of every ten children in our schoolrooms makes his or her way each day through the haze of dangerous psychotropic drugs (drugs that affect the mind).

Millions more don't receive drug therapy, but they are doomed to carry the weight of a negative psychiatric or psychological "diagnosis" that forever labels them as damaged goods and defective persons among their peers. Many may never recover from the long-range effects of such social stigmatizing.

Where did this epidemic come from? What are its causes, and what are its cures? I've heard it said, "Adult questions deserve adult answers." Get ready for some blunt questions and some equally blunt answers based on available factual data. The journey to real solutions may be a bit bumpy as we challenge some of the universally accepted myths embraced and espoused by many health professionals, media sources and educators.

The battle over ADD and our children has produced some serious fractures in the foundation of the American health community. Scientists, respected medical researchers and practitioners and other health professionals are raising a united voice that is questioning the wisdom of the few, the proud and the self-chosen who feel that drugs or psychotherapy are a first response to every problem.

MADE IN AMERICA

It's time to stop applying potentially deadly chemical bandages on our children's symptoms. We should focus our attention and resources on the causes of a child's behavioral or learning problems. I've noticed that most medical professionals tend to overlook or quickly dismiss cultural implications of ADHD and ADD. That seems strange to me since these so-called diseases or mental disorders are essentially unique to North America!

I've been privileged to travel throughout Europe and other countries around the world, where I've found it fascinating to learn about different foods and cultures. I've also studied the foods and lifestyles of different ethnic and people groups, comparing them with key health statistics and death rates. Amazingly, I personally haven't found any evidence of attention deficit disorder in Europe. To my knowledge, the only places in the world where ADD exists in large numbers are Canada and the United States.

The primary treatment for ADD symptoms is the prescription drug Ritalin, which is a Schedule II substance. Schedule II denotes an indexing system that places Ritalin in the same category with methamphetamine, cocaine, morphine, opium, Percodan and Demerol. Most parents of children diagnosed with ADD in America have no idea that Ritalin is such a powerful drug. If your pediatrician told you that your five-year-old needed to go on morphine, would you want a second opinion? (I know I would!)

The DEA and drug enforcement agencies in other nations classify Ritalin as a Schedule II drug because it can be incredibly addictive. Children, adolescents, adults and teachers constantly make the evening news when they grind Ritalin tablets into a fine powder and snort it up their nose as if it were cocaine. Many of them show up in emergency rooms exhibiting the same life-threatening symptoms as those arriving with cocaine overdoses.

FIT FOR SCHOOL,
UNFIT FOR THE MILITARY

The Ritalin puzzle hit the primetime TV circuit on *The Montel Williams Show* and *Dateline NBC*. Not only were audiences shocked to learn that Ritalin has been listed as one of the top ten favorite drugs chosen for pharmaceutical theft in the United States, but how many parents were surprised at discovering that their children who grew up on Ritalin may not be allowed to serve in any branch of the U.S. armed forces? What does the federal government know that it hasn't told us?

It's my personal conviction that certain compelling cultural pressures have helped influence parents in this country to use such strong drugs to control their children.

The social and economic disruption of World War II provided the catalyst for what would become some of the most turbulent years our country has ever experienced during the sixties and seventies. The difficulties of war and economic necessity forced many women out of the home to provide additional revenue for the family.

During the postwar years, Americans began to dream the "American Dream"—owning their own home, parking two cars in the driveway. The problem was that in living this dream Americans changed the way they raised their children. Many young parents were so determined to give their children a better life that they failed to teach them how to work and wait for the things they wanted.

Born on November 8, 1955, I grew up a child of the sixties and seventies. Most of my elementary and secondary school years took place during the most difficult decades of social and spiritual upheaval in the twentieth century. During those decades of change, I made some personal observations.

FREE LOVE, ASSASSINATIONS, PROTEST MARCHES AND DR. SPOCK

I watched the Civil Rights Movement come into its own and national leaders such as President John F. Kennedy, Senator Robert Kennedy and Dr. Martin Luther King, Jr. fall under assassins' bullets. Another fifty-eight thousand Americans died in the rice patties and jungles of Vietnam, a "conflict" that never quite graduated to the dubious status of a war, except perhaps on the battleground of our own soil.

While GIs in Vietnam listened to radios and wished they were home, college students and protesters rioted in the streets of America. Massive protests jammed the streets of Washington as young people demanded an end to the war.

Demonstrators barricaded themselves inside university offices, and National Guard troops shot and killed antiwar demonstrators at Kent State University.

Music was radically transformed into one of the most powerful weapons of the antiwar, antiestablishment movement in the United States. The Woodstock music festival took center stage on the national scene, lending new popularity and status to the hippie movement, "free love" (a.k.a. free sex) and the proliferation of mind-altering drugs.

Prayer was removed from America's schools after the Supreme Court ruled that it violated the so-called "separation clause" of the Constitution, and discipline, rules and self-control were removed from America's homes after Dr. Spock allegedly preached permissive parenting and launched a national paradigm shift in child-rearing.

It wasn't long before "politically correct" thinking and "outcome-based" education were born. That era's legacy also included the dubious blessings of fast-food chains and an entirely new genre of junk food (along with the increased obesity, diabetes, heart disease and cancer statistics that went with it).

STILL REAPING A BITTER HARVEST

The decade of the sixties was an interesting time to be alive, but it sowed some deadly seeds in the American culture that would yield a bitter harvest in future generations. These cultural upheavals directly influenced the sudden emergence of behaviors that later became associated with epidemics and questionable treatments for ADHD, ADD, learning disabilities and autism.

Previously, for the most part, North American culture had been rooted in the European work ethic with a strong commitment to freedom of religion and to Judeo-Christian beliefs. When the social earthquake of the sixties shook the nation, for the first time in two centuries Americans veered away from the social, spiritual and ethical foundations established through more than two thousand years of child rearing. It now embraced more permissive lifestyles and parenting techniques. These accelerated changes exacted a heavy toll on our culture as a whole.

Although many societal changes brought about through the Civil Rights Movement were long overdue, others should have never been tried.

As the principles of permissive parenting swept through the popular and educational culture, the word *no* was deleted in many households. So-called professionals encouraged exasperated parents basically to give their children everything they wanted. In so doing, the youngsters wouldn't suffer from the negative aspects of denial, rejection and the quenching of their natural growth process.

In my opinion, this is one of the reasons so many people in my generation lost their moral compass. When moral absolutes were discarded, promiscuity, drug use, crime and lowered test scores were the results.

Many high school seniors (prime targets for the compulsory draft system of that day) were caught up in the political and social maelstrom that encompassed the Vietnam War. Many of my friends attended college simply to avoid the draft. Others fled to Canada as draft dodgers, while still others protested in the streets and at universities.

Students who dodged the draft by attending college often majored in political science, philosophy and psychology. Four years later while they marched down the aisle to receive their undergraduate degrees, body bags were still arriving from Vietnam. These same college grads burrowed even deeper into the sanctuary of the university system, completing graduate degrees in their respective areas and fields of study.

WELL EDUCATED, INEXPERIENCED AND UNEMPLOYABLE

The war ended in the early seventies, and many well-educated but inexperienced and underprepared social science graduates left the university system seeking work in the private sector. Often these "high thinking" students struggled to find work in their respective fields, so they returned for additional degrees and took teaching positions in the "liberal" universities that had comforted them for so long.

Although numerous and notable exceptions to this scenario exist, approximately 85 percent of college graduates earn degrees that are virtually nonmarketable in a real economy. This is particularly true of advanced social science degrees.

America's liberal education system highly values politically correct thinking. This teaching approach lauds freedom of expression, outcome-based education, situational ethics, little or no corporal discipline for the children and morality-free sexual "education." Such highbrow concepts and "politically correct" policies may sound great on paper. Unfortunately, they offer little practical help for an elementary teacher faced with an overcrowded classroom challenged with a number of out-of-control six- or seven-year-old students.

One rule applies to everyone and everything, no matter who you are or what organization or institution is involved: *The consequences of your actions will always find you out.* To illustrate this point and to inject a little humor in a very serious topic, let me share with you an incident that occurred with my dog Baron.

Any pet owner will tell you that dogs, and higher-level animals in general, share the tendency of children to "hide the evidence" of their wrongdoing from time to time. When Baron decided to run away one time, I took off after him in hot pursuit. It didn't take me long to realize the reason I was falling behind was because he was chasing a female dog.

NECK DEEP AND HIDING THE EVIDENCE

When I finally caught up with Baron at a nearby lake, I saw something I'll never forget. The moment that dog saw me, he "sulkily" waded out into the lake and sat down in neck-deep water with only his ears, eyes and nose sticking out. I suppose he was pretending to be a water ornament or something, just hoping I wouldn't notice him.

When I stopped laughing, I called Baron, and he obediently came out of the water and jumped into the van (and promptly shook himself, divesting himself of at least a half-gallon of muddy lake water in the process). It was obvious to me that the dog knew he had done wrong and his actions had "found him out." (I decided not to fuss at Baron for running away or for giving the interior of my van an unwanted shower because he listened to my command and immediately obeyed, plus he was only doing what came natural to male dogs.)

The point here is, even if a nation does wrong and hides the evidence, the truth will inevitably surface—and the consequences won't be far behind. We have hidden the truth of the 1960s, and the results are upon us with a vengeance.

EMBRACING LEGAL AND ILLEGAL DRUGS

The 1960s spawned a significant drug culture that invaded the arts, the cinema and the social scene. The entire nation has become infected. Today many Americans embrace drugs, both legal and illegal, as the answer to the country's social ills. Prozac, America's favorite designer drug, is hailed as the miracle drug to legally control mood swings. By 1997, it was used by ten to fifteen million people.[7] (Prozac's newer cousins, Zoloft, Luvox and Paxil, probably elevated the number even higher.) Cocaine in many cases has become the illegal drug of choice at parties and on Wall Street.

Given the pervasive tendency to see drugs as the answer in an increasingly permissive society, it was perfectly logical for the medical establishment to suggest drug use as a simple solution for out-of-control children in the classroom. Are your children out of control in the classroom (otherwise defined as having ADD or ADHD)? Give them a pill and don't worry about it. The decision to drug children as a behavioral solution was made without taking into consideration the potential of long-term effects. These include damaged brain development, injured self-esteem and confused understanding that mind-altering drugs are good.

Most of us already know there is a problem. This book is specifically written to give you some positive solutions and some healthful alternatives to using drugs for your children.

ONE

Filtering the Hype From "Attention-Deficit Hyperactivity Disorder"

I f you are confused about attention deficit disorder
(ADD) or attention-deficit hyperactivity disorder
(ADHD), you aren't alone. Psychiatrists and psychologists have invented at least twenty-two names for this ever-
evolving condition, according to the late Robert S.
Mendelsohn, M.D., a practicing pediatrician for thirty years
and one of the nation's leading medical authorities.[1]

The reality of hyperactivity and learning problems
among children is unquestioned. Each year millions of
children and their families face pain and difficulty that are
absolutely genuine. Yet, no single "disease or mental disorder" that is rooted in scientifically established physical or
metabolic abnormalities exists to explain these problems.

In fact, it seems the name of this elusive "disorder"
constantly changes to keep pace with the rapid revisions
(and expansions) of its description. Take your pick of the
favorite names for America's most popular childhood
behavioral diagnosis:

❑ Learning disability (LD)
❑ Minimal brain dysfunction (MBD)

- ❏ Hyperkinetic child syndrome (HCS)
- ❏ Hyperactivity
- ❏ Minor cerebral dysfunction (MCD)
- ❏ Attention deficit disorder (with and without hyperactivity)
- ❏ Attention-deficit hyperactivity disorder (ADHD)
- ❏ Attention-deficit hyperactivity disorder, predominately inattentive type
- ❏ Attention-deficit hyperactivity disorder, predominately hyperactive-impulsive type
- ❏ Attention-deficit hyperactivity disorder, combined[2]

NO PROOF OF DISEASE

Fred A. Baughman, Jr., M.D., a nationally respected board-certified neurologist and child neurologist, asked the U.S. Food and Drug Administration (FDA), the Drug Enforcement Administration (DEA) and leading researchers at the National Institute for Mental Health (NIMH) for scientific proof of physical or chemical abnormalities confirming ADHD as a disease.

The head of the FDA wrote back, "…as yet no distinctive pathophysiology for the disorder has been delineated." Dr. Baughman wasn't surprised when the head of the DEA also stated, "We are also unaware that ADHD has been validated as a biologic/organic syndrome or disease."[3]

According to Dr. Baughman, even the American Psychiatric Association (APA) admits in its *Diagnostic and Statistical Manual of Mental Disorders, Fourth Edition* (*DSM-IV*) that there are "no laboratory tests that have been established as diagnostic" for "attention deficit/hyperactivity disorder." Dr. Baughman told *Insight Magazine*, published by The Washington Times Corporation:

> [ADHD] is a contrived epidemic, where all five million to six million children on these drugs are normal. The

2

country's been led to believe that all painful emotions are a mental illness and the leadership of the APA knows very well that they are representing it as a disease when there is no scientific data to confirm any mental illness.[4]

YOU WON'T BELIEVE THIS

"Don't believe everything you hear," the old saying goes. You are about to discover something I know you won't believe.

Think of each toddler, kindergartner and elementary school student you've raised or observed over the years, and check off the comments that might apply:

- ❑ Often fails to give close attention to details or makes careless mistakes in schoolwork, work or other activities

- ❑ Often has difficulty sustaining attention in tasks or play activities

- ❑ Often does not seem to listen when spoken to directly

- ❑ Often does not follow through on instructions and fails to finish schoolwork, chores or duties in the workplace (not due to oppositional behavior or failure to understand instructions)

- ❑ Often has difficulty organizing tasks and activities

- ❑ Often avoids, dislikes or is reluctant to engage in tasks that require sustained mental effort (such as schoolwork or homework)

- ❑ Often loses things necessary for tasks or activities (e.g., toys, school assignments, pencils, books or tools)

- ❑ Is often easily distracted by extraneous stimuli

❏ Is often forgetful in daily activities

DESCRIBE YOUR KIDS USING THIS LIST

That was easy, wasn't it? Now look at an even shorter list and check the items that accurately describe each kid you are thinking of:

❏ Often fidgets with hands or feet or squirms in seat

❏ Often leaves seat in classroom or in other situations in which it is inappropriate (in adolescents or adults, may be limited to subjective feelings of restlessness)

❏ Often has difficulty playing or engaging in leisure activities quietly

❏ Is often "on the go" or often acts as if "driven by a motor"

❏ Often talks excessively

❏ Often blurts out answers before questions have been completed

❏ Often has difficulty awaiting turn

❏ Often interrupts or intrudes on others (e.g., butts into conversations or games)

Congratulations! I hope you completed the task without excessive fidgeting or grinning. If it is possible, ask your own parents or other close relatives who remember you as a child to compare your early years with these comments.

ACCORDING TO THE "BEST MINDS," YOURS MAY BE DEFECTIVE

Now for the revelation that absolutely amazes me: If you checked just six items in one of these lists, and if those behaviors were observed for a minimum of six months, then according to the best minds in American psychiatry, you or the children you are thinking about may suffer from a mental disorder requiring powerful drug therapy![5]

Don't worry; you will probably be told that two to three pills a day will make the fidgeting go away. (Perhaps I should mention that the pills of choice would probably be a highly addictive cocaine-like drug called Ritalin or an equally powerful amphetamine marketed as Adderall.[6])

You probably hope I'm kidding, but those "diagnostic symptoms" come from the *Diagnostic and Statistical Manual of Mental Disorders, Fourth Edition (DSM-IV)*! As for Ritalin, the side effects of the drug almost exactly duplicate the side effects and dangers of cocaine, amphetamines and methamphetamine.

The International Narcotics Control Board (INCB) reported, "The abuse of methylphenidate [Ritalin] can lead to tolerance and severe psychological dependence. Psychotic episodes [and] violent and bizarre behavior have been reported."[7] One national magazine article noted, "These are, in fact, some of the same symptoms exhibited by Eric Harris" (one of the two shooters behind the Columbine school shootings in 1999).[8]

On the "positive" side, your local emergency room is doubtless well trained to recognize the life-threatening problems and signs of addiction related to Ritalin. Ritalin has become the latest star in the lineup for drug abuse and drug overdose cases in middle-income parties and on college campuses. It even made the DEA's "Top 10" list of most stolen medications![9] (Note: If your child has a true biochemical brain imbalance that causes bizarre behavior, in some cases drug therapy may be necessary.)

IT'S OFFICIAL: NORMAL CHILDHOOD BEHAVIOR IS A DISEASE REQUIRING DRUG TREATMENT

Alarmed? I should think so! Since when has normal childhood behavior been considered a disease? And what debilitating disease deserves treatment with such a dangerous, highly addictive and perception-altering drug? Under normal circumstances where reason prevails, we would imprison or do bodily harm to any adult who tried to drug our children into submission under false pretenses!

The hard truth is that we live in a culture of hype. For the most part, Americans tend to believe what drug companies and doctors are telling us. Kids who don't fit in with the classroom social scene and learning environment are diseased, and Ritalin will rescue them. This is the wonder drug that "saved" ADD Johnny and calmed down ADHD Sally so she can do her homework and give Mommy and Daddy some peace.

If you are one of the millions of people who live with, educate or work with people diagnosed with ADHD or ADD, you need reliable answers to your questions about the nature of ADD symptoms. You also need a clear-eyed, penetrating look at every available solution.

According to all of the evidence, the ADD "symptoms" listed earlier belong to a mental disorder, which is in my opinion fictitious because it was created by a hand vote of the American Psychiatric Association (APA) in 1987. This alleged "psychiatric condition" meets none of the criteria used to determine other diseases by the American Medical Society. In truth, we seem to know more about what ADHD and ADD *is not* than about what it really is.

DOESN'T RITALIN HELP ADD KIDS?

There is absolutely no doubt that Ritalin does something to the human nervous system. So do cocaine, amphetamine, methamphetamine, heroin and methadone, but I wouldn't want to give any of these drugs to my children.

Ritalin may modify a hyperactive child's behavior enough to fit into the rigid format of the typical classroom in the short term, but at what long-term cost? It is also likely to become a lifelong necessity, with a strong possibility of further drug addiction of the worst order.

It would be unthinkable for a doctor or educator to suggest that cocaine, morphine, heroin or methamphetamines be administered to children before each school day. Why doesn't it seem equally as unthinkable that the use of their sister drug, Ritalin, would be as well? I'm convinced that better ways to accomplish the same results exist with no dangerous or life-threatening side effects. It's time we waded through the hype to find some real solutions that don't endanger lives and health.

VIVA LA DIFFERENCE!

As a nutritionist, my clinical practice requires me to understand the role of natural hormones in child development. It makes me wonder if other medical professionals consider the fundamental hormonal differences between little girls and little boys when they diagnose ADHD and ADD? (Or, is that politically incorrect in the realm of mental health services?)

Approximately four out of every five children diagnosed with ADHD or ADD is male. Is it any wonder that more boys than girls match these "symptoms" of so-called disease when the Creator made their bodies to naturally secrete more male hormones to prepare them for their inborn drive to provide and defend? The same hormones that develop masculine secondary sexual characteristics also develop a higher level of drive, aggressive and competitive behavior and difficulty in focusing on slower-paced or passive tasks.

ADHD KIDS: STAND-UP LEADERS IN A SIT-DOWN CLASSROOM CULTURE?

Personally, I have to wonder if it ever occurred to the psychiatric elite that many of the male and female "victims" of this fidget disease may be stand-up leaders who fail to blend into the "sit-down" culture of America's classrooms. No matter: A pill is easier, quicker and far, far, far more profitable!

Sometimes I think that every healthcare student should be forced to attend lengthy and repetitive classes in common sense and basic reasoning. If they are training for psychiatric or psychological practice, they should also major in common sense.

I've noticed several common characteristics among the hyperactive children I've observed or counseled over the years. Obviously not all of these are true in every case, but they seem to be true in many cases.

- ❑ Prenatal nutrition may have been inadequate, including deficiencies in vitamins, minerals, essential fatty acids and supplements.

- ❑ In most cases, the child was bottle-fed and not breast-fed.

- ❑ In many cases, the child was constipated and may have been given laxatives, or he may have been given antacids for gastroesophageal reflux.

- ❑ Many experienced recurring ear and throat infections, while receiving many doses of antibiotics in the process.

- ❑ Many times the child may have been diagnosed with asthma. (By the way, in many cases this condition can be helped if not completely corrected by supplementing the diet with B_5, B_6 and B-complex vitamins.) It is highly probable that

8

the child is taking or has taken amoxicillin (an antibiotic), albuterol (a drug that stimulates bronchodilatation in asthma patients), prednisone (a powerful steroid or glucocorticoid that tends to suppress the immune system and reduce inflammation) or a variety of other drugs.

❑ Sometimes there may have been lead exposure in these children.

❑ Many if not most of the children I observed consumed large amounts of processed foods, including nitrites and red and blue dyes. Children who don't receive proper nutrients in their formative years may be deprived of a proper foundation for a healthful life. (Many of these children lived in a single-parent household.[10] I realize that it is even more difficult for overburdened single parents to provide proper nutrition while also supporting the family and raising children alone. I applaud those who manage to overcome such challenges.)

❑ They are often "latchkey children" who must fend for themselves for many hours each weekday and perhaps all day on weekends because one or both parents are working outside of the home. In some cases, the children even "put themselves to bed."

❑ Very often, but not always, children with behavioral problems have inconsistent parental control and limits placed upon them. At the very least, this component of the home atmosphere must be considered.

❑ These children are often taught to read by using "whole language" rather than phonics.

You are probably thinking, *My child doesn't have all of these problems*. Nevertheless, I'm providing this list to demonstrate how broadly we should spread the diagnostic net to find answers.

PAYING THE PRICE
FOR PARENTAL INDULGENCES?

In working with a variety of clients, I have seen simple dietary modifications greatly impact the distressing behaviors of this ADHD and ADD "epidemic" in children.

The sad reality is that over and over again the children in our society inevitably pay the price for their parents' indulgences. Indulgences such as heavy alcohol consumption, drug abuse and outrageous eating habits may lead to a variety of problems that literally begin in the womb of the mother.

In cases in which a mother receives inadequate vitamins, minerals, folic acid and essential fatty acids during her pregnancy, nutritional deficiencies may produce improper physical and neurological development in her baby.

The good news is that there are some answers that may potentially eliminate hyperactivity or other symptoms associated with attention-deficit hyperactivity disorder and attention deficit disorder—without the potentially serious side effects of psychotropic or psychoactive drugs. That's why I have endeavored to write this book, to provide you the reader and parent with a broader view of ADD, ADHD and autism, and to suggest some options that you may not have considered. For more information on proper eating habits, call my office at (800) 726-1834 and order a copy of my *Eat, Drink & Be Healthy!* program.

TWO

What to Do First: Educate Yourself

If you have been told your child is hyperactive or is suffering from ADHD or ADD, then you probably feel overwhelmed. Take courage. This chapter is for you.

The best cure for hopelessness is information. If your child is having trouble in the classroom, then it's time for you to "go back to school." Educate and arm yourself with knowledge. As you will soon see, in most alleged ADD and ADHD cases, a well-informed parent has a better chance of meeting his or her child's needs than a room full of medical and educational professionals.

Unfortunately, your child's best interests must compete with the self-interests of rushed physicians, profit-driven pharmaceutical companies, frustrated teachers, distracted school administrators, opinionated psychologists and vote-seeking politicians. You alone have the single-minded determination and conflict-free commitment to stand in the maelstrom and demand what is best for your child.

Children depend on us to protect them from harm, to provide for their needs…and to guide them through life's challenges in their formative years. Unfortunately, many "modern" parents have abdicated their parenting role and

11

blindly released their decision-making powers to allegedly "wiser and more knowledgeable decision makers" in institutional settings such as the public school system, the medical community, various faceless governmental bodies and even the pharmaceutical industry.

The pressure to relinquish parental authority is rarely stronger than when we sit before the desk of a pediatrician, psychiatrist, psychologist or professional educator. The sheer psychological weight of impressive academic degrees carefully placed in strategic positions for easy viewing from the "hot seat" makes us feel incredibly uneducated, unprepared and unqualified to question or challenge the words of wisdom uttered from behind that desk. (Have you ever wondered why medical professionals call their customers "patients"? Perhaps it has to do with the patience required by those customers.)

Yet it is precisely in these settings that we must take a stand and demand the right to review the evidence for ourselves. We must protect our freedom to make our own decisions regarding the children we brought into this world.

IT'S A MATTER OF PRIORITIES: WHO CARES THE MOST ABOUT YOUR CHILDREN?

I have no interest in encouraging you to enter into an adversarial relationship with the physicians and educators who work with your children. However, I believe it's important for us parents to preserve our parental authority to make decisions concerning the well-being of our children—even the most complex medical and educational decisions.

The strength of your abilities and argument isn't a matter of education or personal expertise; it is a matter of priorities. No one has your child's best interests in mind the way you do.

One of America's most prominent and controversial pediatricians, Robert Mendelsohn, questioned whether or not his medical specialization was even necessary, noting, "Most childhood illnesses can be treated competently within the home by informed and caring parents. When medical treatment is indicated it can be provided as well by general practitioners or family practitioners or by specialists to whom their patients are referred."[1]

Don't ever let the expertise of professionals intimidate you into believing that their academic training or clinical experience can ever replace the vital force of your unconditional love and innate understanding and wisdom as a parent. No one knows your child as well as you. You have cared for and observed your child virtually every single day since birth.

WOULD YOU TRUST A TEN-MINUTE DIAGNOSIS?

Consider this statement by Dr. Robert S. Mendelsohn the next time you take your child to a healthcare professional:

> Every competent physician knows that 85 percent of an accurate diagnosis is based on the patient's history, 10 percent on a thorough physical examination and the remainder on laboratory tests and x-rays. It takes at least half an hour to take an adequate history and to conduct a thorough physical exam. Pediatricians typically spend 10 minutes with a patient and thus fail to discern much of what they need to know for a reliable diagnosis because they simply don't spend the time that is needed.[2]

If you let them, some experts might tend to discount your parental knowledge and decision-making skills after one hurried interview in a doctor's office or one "psychological screening" session in an artificial environment outside of the home. Wiser healthcare providers would trade one parent's innate understanding for a whole wall full of paper diplomas in most health crisis situations.

A medical school diploma is extremely valuable in life-threatening crisis situations; that's what it's geared for. The flip side is that the very same training may cause a doctor to create a crisis out of a very ordinary physical or mental growth process. For example, the normal process of pregnancy and birth is often treated as if it were a sickness in many modern hospitals and clinics, with medical intervention being the norm rather than the rare exception. This takes the form of numerous unnecessary ultrasound exams, pitocin injections, arbitrary "breaking of the water," occasional forceps deliveries and the pervasive and profitable Cesarean section delivery so popular with doctors who want to "keep a schedule."

Dr. Mendelsohn wrote something in his landmark book *How to Raise a Healthy Child...in Spite of Your Doctor* that continues to stick with me. As a concerned parent, you too may find it worth remembering:

> I have observed, in both the teaching and the practice of medicine, that most doctors do a competent job of treating patients who are very sick and a miserable job of caring for those who are well. This is the major flaw in medical education. The medical student and the pediatric resident, for that matter, learn precious little about how to keep children well, because their education begins with the premise that everyone who comes to their office will require treatment.
>
> ...[The medical school student] absorbs a lot of biased information about immunizations but is taught very little about pharmacology, despite the fact that as a practicing physician he'll hook more kids on drugs than the most diligent pusher in town.[3]

Medical students devote approximately sixty hours to pharmacological studies during their four-year stint in medical school, according to Dr. Mendelsohn. He maintains that most of that time is devoted to irrelevant pharmacological theory. Most of what doctors learn about drugs during their active medical practice comes from the pharmaceutical sales people or "detail men" who stream into their offices with free samples, literature and strong pressure. I'm convinced that most doctors wish only the best for their patients. They really intend to adhere to the first rule of medicine—*primum non nocere*, first do no harm. Nevertheless, I believe that their training for medical crisis can tend to influence their treatment, even when there is no crisis.

Dr. Mendelsohn summed up his discussion of the typical doctor's "hands-on" pharmaceutical training by adding, "If you were to equate this relationship to the distribution of street drugs, the detail man would be the supplier and the doctor the pusher."[4]

DRUGGING "HYPERACTIVE" CHILDREN ON THE STRENGTH OF AN "EDUCATED GUESS"

If you're wondering why I even brought up this subject, think about the epidemic of Ritalin junkies discussed earlier in this book and you will have your answer. Just in case you're not convinced, consider this statement by Dr. Mendelsohn in *Confessions of a Medical Heretic:*

> No modern medical procedure better displays the inquisitorial nature of modern medicine than the drugging of so called "hyperactive" children. Originally, behavior-controlling drugs were used to treat only the most severe cases of mental illness. But today, drugs such as Dexedrine, Cylert, Ritalin, and Tofranil are being used on more than a million children

throughout the United States—on the often flimsy diagnostic criteria of hyperactivity and minimal brain damage. Some medical tests, when performed correctly, are conclusive. But there is no single diagnostic test that will identify a child as hyperactive or any of the twenty-one other names assigned to this syndrome. The list of inconclusive tests is at least as long as the list of names. All a doctor has to go on is a list of inconclusive tests and the "educated" guess of an "expert."[5]

When dealing with medical professionals, never forget that you are the customer and they are vendors providing services. You do not pay them so you will have someone to worship or dictate decisions to you. You pay them to meet specific needs. Furthermore, you reserve the right to find other providers the moment they cease to meet those needs according to your standards.

In her book *No More Ritalin*, Dr. Mary Ann Block shares her and her daughter's experience—an experience similar to what many parents face when they are told their children have ADHD or ADD.[6] When Mary's daughter developed a series of bladder infections (urinary tract infections or UTIs), she did what every other good mother would do— she took her to the doctor. After the fact, Mary remembered her yard had been sprayed with pesticides and that her daughter had developed hives immediately afterward. Since an antihistamine seemed to take care of her daughter's symptoms at the time, she didn't think it mattered.

HE TOLD HER NOT TO READ SO MUCH

The doctor did what doctors often do; he treated the UTIs with drugs (unsuccessfully). Mary had a habit of reading extensively, and she noticed an article that said the drug her doctor prescribed could cause serious neurological damage. When she mentioned it to her daughter's specialist, he told her not to read so much.

A new specialist decided to take a more aggressive approach and placed Mary's daughter on three medications at once: Valium, to "relax the bladder"; Tofranil, an anti-depressant allegedly to stop bedwetting (also used for ADHD symptoms at times); and an antibacterial drug for infection.

Then Mary noticed that Tofranil caused fluid retention, although the specialist said her daughter's problem was that she couldn't excrete all of her urine. Again, Mary's objections were brushed aside because after all, she was just a young mother and not a doctor. Mary said, "Ironically, on this regimen of drugs, my daughter had one of the worst UTIs she had ever experienced. She had hemorrhagic cystitis, which is extremely painful."[7]

Mary mentioned this to her daughter's pediatrician, who became alarmed and told her to stop the drug therapy immediately. When Mary dared to question the doctor about the wisdom of ending Valium doses abruptly and mentioned the symptoms she'd seen when her daughter missed even one dose, the doctor assured her there would be no problems.

ALL THE SIGNS OF
SERIOUS DRUG WITHDRAWAL

Ignoring the warning in the pit of her stomach, Mary faith-fully did what the doctor told her to do. When her daughter began to exhibit serious drug withdrawal symptoms, she called a specialist and was told to wait a few days. She learned later that abrupt withdrawal from Valium can be fatal!

Later on, Mary learned that the combination of three drugs created a toxic cocktail that lowered her daughter's white blood cell count and suppressed her immune system. She went from being a victim of chronic UTIs to suffering from a severe form of mononucleosis. Three years later, Mary's daughter's condition was only worse.

Fed up with the medical circus, Mary finally burrowed into medical literature herself and discovered that the same three-drug cocktail prescribed by the doctors could literally induce a form of mononucleosis that had also been associated with leukemia! When she sounded the alarm, she discovered that most of the doctors involved were more interested in protecting one another than in finding answers for her daughter's health crisis.

Life took a turn for the better when Mary discovered an osteopathic physician. This professional helped her find the underlying cause of her daughter's recurring UTIs and helped the child recover from the toxic poisoning she'd received at the hands of terribly wrong medical specialists.[8] This new physician seemed to approach healthcare in an entirely fresh way. According to Mary:

> He listened to and respected my opinions and input, and educated me by sharing his knowledge. He was a competent and fine physician, with absolutely no arrogance.
>
> But I was still scared about what had been done to my child. I felt that I needed to know what the doctors know to protect my family from anything like this ever happening again. I realized no one was going to care about my family as much as I would.[9]

A CHILLING REMINDER

Mary did what very few of us can do; she enrolled in medical school at the age of thirty-nine and ultimately became an osteopathic physician! Dr. Mary Ann Block built a very successful medical practice drawing from her experiences as an exasperated mother seeking answers. She said, "…the current trend of treating ADHD symptoms with serious drugs is a chilling reminder of the once acceptable treatment used on [my daughter]."[10]

You don't necessarily have to become a doctor to protect your children or make informed decisions about their healthcare and education, but you do need to educate yourself. There is a wealth of information available to you in your local library, in magazines and on the Internet. If you are serious about educating yourself, then you may want to purchase your own copy of the *Physicians' Desk Reference (PDR)*, the "doctor's Bible" of information about diseases, drugs and physical symptoms.[11]

Be slow to accept any diagnosis for your children or yourself that doesn't "ring true" to you. God gave you parental instincts for a good reason (some would say it was to protect your children from "quackery"). You may find it useful to use Dr. Mendelsohn's excellent three-point guideline for diagnosis from *How to Raise a Healthy Child...in Spite of Your Doctor:*

1. If your child doesn't feel sick, look sick and act sick, he probably isn't sick.

2. Give Mother Nature ample time to work her magic before you expose your child to the potential physical and emotional side effects of treatments that your doctor may administer. The human body has a remarkable capacity to heal itself—a capacity that in most cases surpasses anything that medical science can do—and it doesn't produced unwanted side effects.

3. Common sense is the most useful tool in dealing with illness. Your doctor is less likely to employ it than you are, and certainly no more able, because that's not what they taught him in medical school![12]

FIND A COMPETENT
HEALTHCARE PROVIDER

One of your most important tasks as a responsible parent is to find a competent and trustworthy healthcare provider. It took Mary Ann Block several years to find a physician she could trust who treated her as a partner in the care of her daughter. I recommend that you find a healthcare provider who does the following:

❑ Listens to what you have to say about your child's symptoms, behavior, motivations and habits. Make sure he or she also listens to your personal convictions, thoughts, hunches or conclusions about your child's situation.

❑ Asks questions about your child's health, situation, learning style, eating habits and daily nutrition, play style, interpersonal relationships, drug and food sensitivities, allergies and so forth.

❑ Takes time to share knowledge with you about any area possibly related to your child's physical, mental or social well-being. He or she should share this knowledge in a way that makes you feel accepted, not as a second-rate nuisance who is taking up valuable time.

❑ Is willing to *admit* his or her *knowledge is limited.* Do everything you can to avoid any healthcare provider suffering from the dreaded "messiah syndrome." This affliction makes it virtually impossible for many physicians, surgeons and other healthcare providers to admit a mistake or a lack of knowledge.

Since the first choice of many "experts" who routinely label children with the ADHD or ADD diagnosis is drug therapy, you should also develop a good relationship with a pharmacist in your area. Make sure you ask him for detailed information about any drug prescribed to your family members before you purchase it. Ask for any available information about how the drug interacts with other medications—prescribed and over-the-counter (OTC) drugs—with foods, with vitamin supplements and with environmental elements such as exposure to direct sunlight.

While some parents of children diagnosed with ADHD or ADD feel comfortable sharing about their children, many do not. Seek out or develop a support network of other parents whose children have been diagnosed with learning disorders. Freely share the information provided in this book and in other authoritative sources you've discovered in your self-education effort.[13]

CONSIDER ALL THE EVIDENCE

By its very nature, the education process is "open-ended." So, examine and consider all the evidence concerning ADHD, ADD, autism or any other area of research. Make sure you gather information from many sources, not just a few.

I firmly believe that we have nothing to fear from science—it merely reflects the qualities and principles of God's creation. However, I do not believe in the scientific infallibility of the medical profession. Many years of university undergraduate and graduate training in nutrition and biochemistry, as well as more than two decades of clinical experience as a nutritionist and researcher, have taught me to exercise great caution when interpreting scientific data.

Accurate answers can only be obtained by properly framing our questions and investigation methods. Since human beings are highly skilled at framing their questions and skewing their methodology to arrive at conclusions of their own choosing, you must proceed with caution if you choose to step beyond the boundaries of politically correct thinking about ADHD and ADD.

In the interest of integrity, we will consider both the pros and the cons of the latest information available. We'll examine research and recommendations for drug therapy, psychiatric testing and diagnosis procedures, psychological therapy and public policy toward ADHD, ADD and other key healthcare issues. Nevertheless, as always, the choices are yours to make.

When you complete the last chapter you will be equipped with the basic knowledge you need to find your own answers. I'm not asking you to trust me; I want you to trust yourself. Have confidence in your own ability to conduct the research, evaluate the available data and make a quality decision.

DISCUSS THE FACTS, DISMISS THE MYTHS

If you feel poorly equipped to discuss Ritalin therapy with a school administrator, then do what it takes to master the material. Remember that most doctors get their information about Ritalin from drug detailers or from the *Physicians' Desk Reference (PDR)*, which is written on an eighth-grade reading level. All you need is a good dictionary and the discipline to read through the material. At the end of the quest, you will be well equipped to discuss the facts and authoritatively dismiss the myths.

If you feel poorly prepared to counter your school district's mandate that you medicate your child or leave him home, just educate yourself. You aren't the first, but you may have the potential to be the last victim of such an unconstitutional directive if you educate yourself and arm yourself with knowledge for the conflict. The battle for your child's safety, well-being and best interests begins and ends with you.

THREE

Ritalin—Educating the Medicated: Why Do We Drug Our Kids?

Every school day, America's future files into the halls of public school buildings to receive the education allegedly designed to help these kids succeed as adults. Nearly one out of every ten students starts his or her day with "the breakfast of champions"—these youngsters take the same kind of addictive psychoactive drugs that street dealers will steal or kill for.[1]

If you are thinking, *It should be a crime!*, then I have to agree with you. But how do we convince our children's drug suppliers to agree as well? Drug therapy is just too easy, trouble-free and profitable compared to the cost and effort of finding real answers to underlying problems in these children and adults.

The ease of it all may be our greatest and most insurmountable problem. The popularity of Ritalin with school administrators and some parents of ADHD and ADD children has very little to do with chance.

The manufacturers of Ritalin and its long-term release cousins, Concerta and Metadate, have poured millions of dollars into mass promotion programs aimed at CHADD (Children and Adults with Attention Deficit Disorder), the

educational and medical communities and the public—
sometimes with embarrassing results.

The DEA had already begun to consider an interesting
petition presented by CHADD and cosigned by the
American Academy of Neurology. It urged that Ritalin be
removed from the heavily restricted and monitored drug
classification it shares with amphetamines and morphine
when a political bombshell hit the media.

THE BUSINESS OF PUTTING PROFIT
AHEAD OF CHILD SAFETY

Both the government agency and the academy were caught
off-guard in 1995 when the United Nations and the DEA
released a report after conducting a yearlong investigation
of alleged financial ties between Ciba-Geigy (then the
manufacturer of Ritalin) and CHADD. Officials publicly
expressed their concern that the relationship "may be
putting profit margins ahead of child safety."[2]

The DEA report claimed that the drug manufacturer had
contributed nearly one million dollars to the high-profile
parent advocacy group. At the time, CHADD was lobbying
to have Ritalin reclassified or downgraded to a less restricted
drug classification to make it cheaper and more accessible.
(Evidently, the right hand of the DEA—the part concerned
with setting regulations standards—didn't know what the
left hand—the one that does the watchdog work—was
doing.) Even the International Narcotics Control Board
expressed its concern over the lobbying effort to move
Ritalin beyond the control of strict prescription guidelines.

A report in *USA Today* included an interview with Gene
Haislip, then DEA's head of diversion control:

> Haislip says CHADD literature "misleads" members
> about Ritalin's safety while Ciba's profits rose from
> $50 million to $108 million in recent years. "Looks to

me like a lot of factors have pushed this out of balance," he says of what he calls the "unhealthy comingling of medical and commercial interests."[3]

The same article reported that when the U.S. Department of Education learned about the financial ties between Ciba-Geigy and CHADD in late in 1995, the department immediately recalled a $100,000 video produced by CHADD that had already been distributed to educators around the nation eight months earlier.

NIMH: NO PROOF THAT DRUGS HELP KIDS IN THE LONG RUN

Ironically, a large NIMH (National Institutes of Mental Health) study that appeared in the *Archives of General Psychiatry* in 1999 indicated that while powerful stimulant drugs like Ritalin may calm down some ADHD kids, *"there's no proof that in the long run the drugs help kids get better grades or build better lives."*[4] Perhaps CHADD should reconsider its information and move some of its ideas from the realm of "scientifically proven facts" to the file labeled "myths to dismiss."

The relationship between the manufacturer of Ritalin and CHADD has been well documented and publicly acknowledged by both parties for many years. However, serious questions about Novartis's (the current manufacturer of Ritalin) heavy promotion of Ritalin and suspicion that another party had joined the mutually beneficial relationship evidently triggered four separate Federal lawsuits in California, Texas, Florida and New Jersey.

During his testimony before the congressional subcommittee panel, Dr. Breggin said he was scheduled to testify as an expert witness in the four civil suits alleging that Novartis had committed fraud by overpromoting ADHD and Ritalin. He said the suits "also charge Novartis with conspiring with the American Psychiatric Association (APA) and with CHADD, a parents' group that receives money from the pharmaceutical industry and lobbies on its behalf." Three of the lawsuits were class action suits (two national and one for the State of California), and the fourth was a California business fraud action.[5]

As of this writing, a federal judge in California has dismissed the California lawsuit on grounds that the claim violated California's anti-SLAPP (Strategic Lawsuits Against Public Participation) legislation. In other words, the judge felt the activities of Novartis, CHADD and the APA were protected speech under the free speech guarantees of the U.S. and California constitutions. The judge left the door open for the plaintiffs to amend their complaint, but warned them to come forward with sufficient evidence.[6]

GROWING DISSATISFACTION

Despite the difficulty of proving conspiracy in a court of law, it is likely that such attempts to curtail the profitable relationship between the drug manufacturer, CHADD and the American Psychiatric Association will continue because of what Dr. Breggin called "a growing dissatisfaction with the drugging of millions of children."[7]

Whether we believe an alliance exists or whether we simply dismiss it as another conspiracy theory, something seems to be motivating parents to line up at their neighborhood pharmacy for Johnny's going-to-school drug. According to a 1999 report issued by the *Archives of Pediatrics and Adolescent Medicine*, "Youth doctor visits for ADHD increased 90 percent from 1989 to 1996." Even more alarming was the fact that *more than 75 percent of those children between the ages of five and fourteen were prescribed drugs (mainly stimulants) for that condition!*[8]

The probability is that very few parents of children diagnosed with ADHD or ADD and prescribed Ritalin really understand that stimulant medications have been shown to seriously retard or stop growth processes in the young, causing major organs of the body to simply stop growing.

COUNTING THE COST

Dr. Peter Breggin told a congressional subcommittee that stimulants have the capacity to permanently change brain chemistry, a property that carries considerable risk for young children and adolescents.

> Animals and humans cross-addict to methylphenidate [marketed as Ritalin, Concerta, and Metadate], amphetamine [Dexedrine and Adderall], and cocaine. These drugs affect the same three neurotransmitter systems and the same parts of the brain...
>
> Studies of amphetamine show that short-term clinical doses produce *brain cell death*. Similar studies of methylphenidate show long-lasting and sometimes permanent changes in the biochemistry of the brain.
>
> *All stimulants impair growth* not only by suppressing appetite but also by disrupting growth hormone production. This poses a threat to *every organ of the body, including the brain*, during the child's growth. The disruption of neurotransmitter systems adds to this threat.
>
> These drugs also endanger the cardiovascular system and commonly produce many adverse mental effects, including depression.[9]

According to Tony Tommasello, director of the office of substance abuse studies at the University of Maryland's School of Pharmacy, teenagers abused Ritalin in the 1970s. The drug provided an increased sense of self-confidence, enhanced mental alertness and energy along with an increase in blood pressure and heart rate.

THERE'S A PRICE TO PAY

Tommasello added, "These things feel good, but when the drug wears off, there's a price to pay, including depression, apathy, loss of concentration and memory. Ritalin is as dangerous as the use of any other stimulant. Continued use over long periods, or taken in a single large dose, Ritalin can produce disastrous results, including heart attack and stroke."[10]

These facts appeared to be conveniently forgotten several years ago when several research studies (mostly using small numbers of subjects) proudly announced that brain scans of boys diagnosed with ADHD and ADD revealed that three suspect areas of their brains were allegedly smaller than those of "normal" boys.

The results of the first larger study completed in 1995 by the National Institutes of Mental Health (NIMH) were publicly announced before the approving members of CHADD who had gathered in Washington, DC, for the advocacy group's annual convention.

One news report issued the same day claimed that the study "added to evidence that ADHD has a neurobiological cause." The study involved 112 boys between the ages of four and eighteen, half of whom had been diagnosed with ADHD.

Evidently the study had one very serious design flaw. A *USA Today* report said that when questioned, the researchers who conducted the NIMH study reluctantly admitted that "the structural brain differences detected *could have been caused by the drug's use*...even though the boys they studied had been drug-free for four weeks." The NIMH study was four times larger than any previous investigation.[11]

It is said that "hope springs eternal," but determined researchers with an agenda seem to give a new meaning to eternal hope. Three years later, Stanford University researchers once again announced that they had found differences in brain activity in children who have been diagnosed with attention deficit disorder. The same *USA Today* reporter who reported the NIMH findings years before, Karen Thomas, dutifully reported the Stanford findings (while no doubt thinking she was experiencing *déjà vu*).

RITALIN USE MAY HAVE AFFECTED BRAIN SCANS

The study was based on a paltry sample of only sixteen male subjects between the ages of eight and thirteen years. Once again the report acknowledged a key factor: "The ten boys who had been diagnosed with ADD had been taking Ritalin for one to three years before researchers studied them, and no one knows how the boys' drug use may have affected the brain scans."[12]

Perhaps the coincidence was meaningless. Yet, the researchers' report had been released in the Proceedings of the National Academy of Sciences "just days after a government panel concluded that doctors have *no consistent physical way* to identify ADD or diagnose who has it."[13]

These frequent admissions concerning the possible effects of Ritalin on brain development effectively invalidate the conclusion that ADD brains were smaller than normal. Sadly, the myth of a biological cause lives on, and the drugging of kids continues to escalate.

Nevertheless, those who advocate the use of stimulant drugs as the treatment of choice continue to claim that ADHD is caused by unspecified changes in the brain. The myth persists even though two respected medical organizations were forced to refute the claims.

ABNORMALITIES CAUSED BY MEDICATION?

According to Dr. Breggin, "Both the NIH [National Institute for Health] Consensus Development Conference

(1998) and the American Academy of Pediatrics (2000) report on ADHD have confirmed that there is no known biological basis for ADHD. Any brain abnormalities in these children are almost certainly caused by prior exposure to psychiatric medication."[14]

One lesson to be learned here might be that if you don't want your child to go through life with a potentially smaller-sized brain, then keep him away from Ritalin and those who like to prescribe it. A second lesson is anything but new: Don't believe everything you are told—even if the source is wearing a lab coat and pocket protector. Dare to dig deeper for all the evidence.

We may not know the causes of the supposed disorders labeled as ADHD or ADD. And we may not understand the pharmacology of Ritalin and amphetamines, but there is no doubt about their effects.

> Hundreds of animal studies and human clinical trials leave no doubt about how the medication works.
>
> First, the drugs suppress all spontaneous behavior [sic, "abnormal behavior" in the typical American dumbed-down classroom]. In healthy chimpanzees and other animals, this can be measured with precision as a reduction in all spontaneous or self-generated activities. In animals and humans, this is manifested in a reduction in the following behaviors: (1) exploration and curiosity, (2) socializing, and (3) playing.
>
> Second, the drugs increase obsessive-compulsive behaviors, including very limited, overly focused activities.[15]

THESE AREN'T IMPROVEMENTS— THEY ARE TOXIC SIDE EFFECTS!

Dr. Breggin asserts that many of the adverse stimulant effects produced by the drugs prescribed to school children are commonly mistaken as "improvements" by clinicians, teachers and parents.

One of the biggest problems with such overt approval of drug therapy is that officials in public institutions and medical communities aren't necessarily recognized for their appreciation of freedom of choice by parents of so-called "problem students."

The Boston Globe reported the plight of two families allegedly pressured by school officials in Lawrence, Massachusetts, to place their children on Ritalin.

One parent filed a civil rights complaint against the school district saying the district pressured her to put her son back on Ritalin and failed to offer him adequate classroom support when she refused. Officials from the U.S. Department of Education's civil rights division were expected to arrive in Lawrence within a week to investigate the allegation.

Another parent stepped forward and said he planned to file a similar complaint against the Lawrence school district with the Department of Education. The school district superintendent denied the charges, but assigned an aide to one of the boys and placed the other in a special classroom. He also warned teachers and administrators to avoid pressuring parents about Ritalin use.[16]

Public pressure apparently forced this particular school district to back away from heavy-handed control tactics, but that doesn't even begin to make a dent in the broader problem.

WILL YOUR CHILD JOIN THE SIX TO SEVEN MILLION KIDS ALREADY TAGGED WITH A PSYCHIATRIC DISORDER?

According to the Citizens Commission on Human Rights (CCHR), a nonprofit international watchdog organization that monitors psychiatric and psychological abuses worldwide, at least six million American children have been diagnosed with a "psychiatric disorder" of some form that requires medication. If you want to know how that happened, consider the first sentence of CCHR's next statement:

> Under criteria voted on by the APA, any child can be diagnosed as having "Attention Deficit Disorder" (ADD) or "Attention Deficit Hyperactivity Disorder" (ADHD). The criteria for "ADHD" consists of 18 points, including "has difficulty playing quietly," "often talks excessively" and "often loses things."[17]

Based on these criteria, perhaps we should ask who *wouldn't* be diagnosed with ADHD or ADD during childhood! That is a frightening thought for any parent of school-age children—after all, *any* child could include *your* child.

You examined the diagnosis criteria for yourself at the beginning of the previous chapter. Now link the extreme normality of those "symptom" lists with the fact that the ADHD and ADD diagnosis is entirely subjective. The examiner must rely on his or her own personal ideas of what is "normal" behavior for your child while filtering out whether or not they are having a "bad day."

Many children are diagnosed with ADHD each year by school psychologists who are paid by the school districts they serve. What standards of behavior do you think the average school psychologist tends to bring into any subjective examination of your child? Is he or she generally more concerned with maintaining the status quo in the school district or with finding the best possible solutions for your child's learning styles, personality, abilities and needs? Which is easier?

When a child transfers to another school district or moves up a grade, the stigma of any ADHD or ADD diagnosis—

and any medication prescribed by a doctor—goes with him. It is routine for a doctor to notify your child's school if any medication has been prescribed for ADHD or ADD, and school officials are expected to communicate details of your child's performance to the doctor.

You may perceive this as a good thing since it might help the doctor properly monitor the effects of the medication. But consider how much parental authority and privacy have been firmly yanked away from you in the process.

"EXPANSION"

As dangerous as Ritalin or other stimulants such as Dexedrine and Adderall (known on the street as "dexies" or simply "speed") may be to your child's health and well-being, the latest trend in childhood disorder diagnosis and psychotropic therapy for ADHD will give you even more to worry about! The key word to understand is *expansion*.

Doctors seem to be embracing two interactive trends that could very well threaten the lives of the increasingly younger patients. According to Lawrence H. Diller, M.D., who practices behavioral pediatrics in the San Francisco area:

> Diagnosing bipolar disorder in children as young as three has become the latest rage. It justifies using a host of meds to treat very difficult-to-manage, unhappy children. The old-line drug, lithium, has been replaced by newer, untested (in children) mood stabilizers like Neurontin or Depakote as a first-choice intervention for pediatric "manic depression." Finally, a new class of anti-psychotic medications—the most popular these days is Risperdal—is heralded as the ultimately effective treatment for a number of diagnoses whose common features are not hallucinations or psychosis, but several acting-out behaviors.[18]

MADE IN AMERICA!

Noting that "…no other society prescribes psychoactive medications to children the way we do," Dr. Diller said, "Psychiatrists in [Europe and industrialized Asia] are perplexed and worried about trends in America. The use of psychoactive drugs other than Ritalin for preteen children is virtually unheard of outside this country."[19] (As I mentioned earlier, I have never seen its use in Europe.)

The process of expanding a diagnosis is simple. (The following scenario is based on an actual treatment history of a child prior to his arrival at Dr. Diller's office.) Once a physician diagnoses ADD or ADHD and prescribes a stimulant such as Ritalin to "calm down" a child or help him focus, very often the youngster develops one or more of the behavioral side effects so common to long-term stimulant use. These may include the inability to sleep well, increased irritability or signs of depression. That leads to a second or even a third medication to counteract those symptoms. The usual choice is an antidepressive drug such as Wellbutrin (used to treat depression and anorexia nervosa in adults) and a powerful "sleep aid" such as Anafranil (originally used to treat adult depression and obsessive-compulsive disorder—but generally avoided because most people felt too sedated by the drug).

If the same child continues to exhibit behavioral problems, the treatments spiral downward. If the youngster is examined by a growing number of psychiatrists who firmly believe that serious mental illnesses are common in childhood, he or she may well be diagnosed with bipolar disorder. Bipolar disorder is a new term for manic-depressive disorder. Now, a fifth prescribed medication, called Neurontin, can be added, an anticonvulsant conveniently renamed a "mood stabilizer."[20]

WHAT HARM WILL COME?

The sad truth is that children as young as three years old are being subjected to these mind-altering drugs, and no one—including the prescribing physicians—knows what these psychotropic drug cocktails will do to young developing brains.

William G. Crook, M.D., noted pediatrician, allergist and immunologist, cited a study appearing in the *Journal of the American Academy of Child and Adolescent Psychiatry*. It found that hyperactive boys treated with stimulant medication—even those receiving a comprehensive program of psychological and educational therapy, "were prone to use marijuana and alcohol and engage in vandalism and petty theft."[21]

The technical name for the trend of prescribing multiple prescriptions is *combined pharmacotherapy*. The favorite name used by health professionals who disapprove of the practice is *polypharmacy*.[22]

Dr. Diller was shocked to find that between 1995 and 1999, doctors' use of stimulant drugs on children rose 23 percent; the use of Prozac-like drugs for children of ages seven through twelve rose 151 percent, and for children age six or younger, it rose 580 percent![23]

GOOD NEWS FOR INVESTORS: MOOD STABILIZER PRESCRIPTIONS FOR MINORS UP 4,000 PERCENT!

Dr. Diller also learned that "for children under the age of eighteen, the use of 'mood stabilizers' other than lithium is up forty-fold, or 4,000 percent, and the use of new antipsychotic medications such as Risperdal has grown nearly 300 percent"![24] This is alarming news in its own right. The picture grows even darker and more ominous when you realize that many doctors are blending one or more of these dangerous drugs into psychotropic cocktails with little if any research to predict their effects on our children!

The problem becomes virtually overwhelming when you factor in the popular practice of off-label prescription of medications for purposes for which they were never designed or tested. Once the FDA approves a drug for any use, doctors have carte blanche power to prescribe it "off label" any way they want. "Virtually every other med used to treat children's behavior is prescribed this way," according to Dr. Diller. "Off-label use of medicines in pediatrics is common, but nowhere more so than in psychiatric medications."[25]

The most popular ingredients favored by medical bartenders for psychotropic cocktails include SSRIs (new antidepressant drugs called "serotonin selective reuptake inhibitors") such as Prozac, Paxil and Luvox. Prescribing SSRI antidepressants like Prozac in addition to Ritalin is getting more popular with doctors, but does it work? Dr. Diller said, "…the one study demonstrating the effectiveness of Prozac in children when the patients and doctors didn't know which pill was taken, *60 percent of the improvement in depressive symptoms* was attributed to the *placebo effect*."[26]

(A placebo is a neutral "fake" medicine that has no true effect on the subject. Placebo pills are usually given to one group of patients without their knowledge, while the real drug is given to another group. Physicians and pharmaceutical companies hate to see a placebo outperform their test drug.)

Also popular are antipsychotic drugs or "mood stabilizers" like Risperdal, Depakote, Neurontin and the older drug lithium (all with far more serious side effects than Ritalin), and adult blood pressure medications such as clonidine and Tenex.

PSYCHIATRIC GUINEA PIGS?

Few of these drugs have been tested on children. One FDA official made a statement that should send a chill down the back of every caring parent whose child has been labeled ADHD or ADD and prescribed medication.

Noting that children are not miniature adults, Thomas Laughren, the director of the FDA team that approves psychiatric medications, said, "They're going through a lot of physiological changes that probably make them more vulnerable to the effects of drugs." Adding that the most popular drugs alter brain chemistry and the long-term effects are unknown, Laughren concluded, "We just don't have enough information to draw the conclusion that they're safe and effective for children."[27]

Once a child falls into the "expanded diagnosis" of ADHD with bipolar disorder, virtually anything goes in the psychotropic prescription game.

One psychiatrist cynically remarked, "Ritalin is for irritable and irritating children while lithium is for very irritable and very irritating children."[28]

According to Dr. Diller, "More than 200,000 children receive anti-psychotic medications [such as lithium], mostly to control unruly behavior rather than to treat hallucinations or other symptoms of schizophrenia."[29] He goes on to say:

> The number of children combining two or more psychoactive drugs is unknown. Combined pharmacotherapy (known pejoratively as polypharmacy) has been strongly endorsed by leading research groups as the sensible approach to treating the co-morbid, or multiple occurring, diagnoses common in "high problem resistant behavior" children. Some doctors call it prescribing by "symptom chasing."[30]

THE ONLY SOLUTION?

The picture is dismal if you believe everything you hear, especially if you believe the pharmaceutical propaganda flooding the school systems and permeating parent advocacy groups that claim drug therapy is the only way to go. It isn't.

Dr. Peter Breggin may be considered a maverick among his peers in the psychiatric profession, but his credentials, ethics and medical skills were valued enough for his appointment by the National Institutes of Health. He was named to a panel of top medical experts invited to present peer-reviewed scientific papers and participate in the prestigious 1998 NIH Consensus Development Conference on the Diagnosis and Treatment of Attention-Deficit Hyperactivity Disorder. I think this very unusual psychiatrist should have the last word in this chapter devoted to the largely uncontrolled family of psychotropic drugs and their misuse on children:

> In my private practice, children can often be taken off all psychiatric drugs (only under careful medical supervision) with great improvement in their psychological life and behavior, provided that the parents or other interested adults are willing to learn new approaches to disciplining and caring for the children. Consultations with the school, a change of teachers or schools, and home schooling can also help meet the needs of children without resorting to medication.[31]

FOUR

Do Treatments
Pass or Fail?

Since every ADHD and ADD diagnosis made in America seems to follow guidelines created by psychiatry, then the philosophical bases, history, procedures, claims and track record of psychiatry must stand the test of close inquiry. After all, the well-being of millions of young lives is riding on the reputation and expertise of the psychiatric discipline.

We begin with the well-established fact that ADD and ADHD did not exist as a disease or disorder until 1987 when the American Psychiatric Association voted it into existence.

Perhaps you are wondering, *What do you mean they "voted" ADHD into existence? Is that what doctors normally do?*

Unlike other medical disciplines, many psychiatric diseases and disorders appear to have no scientifically proven source, cause or definitive tests.

A U.S. Congressional Office of Technology Assessment Report issued in 1992 said, "Research has yet to identify specific biological causes for any of these [mental] disorders... Mental disorders are classified on the basis of symptoms because there are as yet no biological markers or laboratory tests for them."[1]

Four years later, psychiatrist David Kaiser said, "Modern psychiatry has yet to convincingly prove the genetic/biologic cause of any single mental illness."[2]

This fact hasn't changed, even though we are well into another millennium at this writing.

STILL GROPING AFTER ALL THESE YEARS...

The Citizens Commission on Human Rights (CCHR), an internationally recognized watchdog group, issued this blistering indictment of psychiatry in a heavily researched article released in 2000:

> After 150 years, psychiatry still has absolutely no understanding of, or cure for, insanity or mental problems. It has never scientifically isolated any root cause of mental problems, has no proof whatsoever to back its claim of a biological or genetic cause of mental "illness," has no understanding of how psychoactive drugs, electroshock or lobotomies affect the mind, has zero ability to predict human behavior or prevent the onset of mental problems, and has no valid clue on what constitutes good mental health or how to create it.[3]

Perhaps the most serious indictments of psychiatry come from dissenting professionals within the psychiatric ranks. Dr. Thomas Szasz, professor emeritus of psychiatry, claims that psychiatry is "the single most destructive force that has affected ... society within the last fifty years." He also said, "The designation 'disease' can only be justified when the cause can be related to a demonstrable anatomical lesion, infection or some other physiological defect."[4]

Evidently, since there is no such evidence for ADHD or ADD, the use of the terms "mental disorder" and "disease" are totally incorrect, socially stigmatizing for children and may even be fraudulent. As Edward Shorter notes with unusually blunt insight in his book *A History of Psychiatry: From the Era of the Asylums to the Age of Prozac,* "Psychiatrists have an obvious self-interest in pathologizing human behavior..."[5]

IF IN DOUBT, VOTE

In contrast to the rigid standards generally followed by the rest of the medical world when isolating a designated disease, the American Psychiatric Association didn't designate ADHD as a mental disorder because the brain structure, central nervous systems or genes of "ADHD children" were different from "normal" kids—because they aren't different; they are the same.

The truth is that there is "no biological marker, no brain scan, no blood test, no definitive psychological test that absolutely diagnoses ADHD."[6] ADHD became a "disorder" by an arbitrary vote of the APA, not through any scientific deliberation over established facts.

The CCHR says of the *DSM-IV*: "Arrived at by what psychiatrists call 'consensus,' which in reality is no more scientific or sophisticated than a vote of insider hands, the *DSM-IV* contains a record 374 so-called mental disorders..."[7] (ADHD is just one of those "products of consensus.")

Biopsychologist Elliot S. Valenstein, author of *Blaming the Brain*, said, "*DSM-IV* is not an exciting document. It is purely descriptive and presents no new scientific insights or any theories about what causes the many mental disorders it lists."[8]

John Leo pulled no punches in his On Society column "Doing the Disorder Rag" for *U.S. News & World Report*:

> The *DSM* is converting nearly all of life's stresses and bad habits into mental disorders. Almost everything we feel or do is listed somewhere in the *DSM* as an indicator of some dread disorder...

Psychiatrists are free to declare as many people disordered as they wish. But the effort and the concepts behind this are seeping deep into the culture, reinforcing the victim industry and teaching us to look for psychiatric answers to every social and personal problem.[9]

THE STRANGE JOURNEY

Unfortunately, this process has everything to do with ADHD, ADD and our children. Most thinking adults are taken aback when they probe the strange journey of ADHD and psychiatry's treatment of choice—drug therapy—into America's elementary and kindergarten classrooms. Examine this chronology of events and draw your own conclusions:

❑ 1801—Johann Christian Reil, who first coined the word *psychiatry*, described what some believe is still the central purpose of the profession, especially in its efforts to bring mass chemical control to America's classrooms: "Through strong, painful impressions we capture the patient's attention, accustom him to unconditional obedience, and indelibly imprint in his heart the feeling of necessity. The will of his superior must be such a firm, immutable law for him that he will no more resist it than he would rebel against the elements."[10]

❑ 1861—President Abraham Lincoln decided to stop taking his doctor's prescription for "blue mass," the established treatment for melancholia at that time. It is a good thing he did. Researchers discovered in 2001 that each of the blue antidepressant pills contained four times the daily limit for mercury "along with licorice root, rose water, dead rose petals, honey and sugar." The recommended dose of two or three pills per day was potent enough to kill him. Lincoln was troubled with fits of rage, insomnia and tremors, but all of these classic symptoms of mercury poisoning evidently ended when his "treatment" ended. This was one patient who unwittingly escaped the dangers of early psychiatric drug therapy and probably saved the United States of America from destruction by division, although he was assassinated four years later.[11]

❑ 1865—Zurich psychiatrist Wilhelm Griesinger claimed that since most of the nerve coverage was in the brain, *all mental problems* must be *diseases* of the brain (emphasis mine).[12]

❑ 1879—Psychologist Professor Wilhelm Wundt of Leipzig University in Germany declared that there was no soul and that man was simply a higher level animal that could be controlled using "science."[13]

❑ 1930s—Within a five-year period in this decade, insulin coma, metrazol shock, electroshock and lobotomies were widely prescribed by psychiatrists worldwide. While all caused physical damage to the patient, none ever effected a cure.[14]

❑ 1946—The United States psychiatric research body, National Institute of Mental Health (NIMH), was established with psychiatrist Dr. Robert Felix as its first director.[15]

❑ 1952—The APA publishes the first edition of the *Diagnostic and Statistical Manual of Mental Disorders (DSM)*, listing 112 mental maladies with recommended "treatments" but no definitive causes or cures.

❑ 1963—The Community Mental Health Centers Act implemented "de-institutionalization"—the emptying of state psychiatric hospitals that sent drugged patients homeless into the streets. This was facilitated by the discovery of tranquilizing (antipsychotic) drugs.[16] (According to Dr. Thomas Szasz, professor emeritus of psychiatry, "The insane person could now be controlled with a chemical, instead of a mechanical, straitjacket: The restraint could be put in him, instead of on him."[17])

❑ 1965—The U.S. Elementary and Secondary Education Act becomes law, expanding the definition of "handicapped" to include "mental disturbance."

❑ 1968—The second edition of *Diagnostic and Statistical Manual of Mental Disorders (DSM-II)* appears, including for the first time a new category called "Behavior Disorders of Childhood and Adolescence." (Is this a case of mere coincidence or of "opportunistic expansion" in response to the education act passed in 1965?)

❑ 1975—Individuals with Disabilities Education Act (IDEA) becomes law, mandating and underwriting "special education" classes for children with "learning disabilities." (Note: The idea of providing special services to individuals with disabilities is a fine idea—the apparently unscientific creation of "mental diseases" by consensus and labeling children with "learning disorders" is not.)

❑ 1977—The number of children labeled as having "learning disorders" (LDs) suddenly and mysteriously mounts to 782,000. (Within twelve years, it would rise to 1.9 million. By 1996, the number was at 2.6 million!)

❏ 1987—The APA "votes" into existence a new mental "disorder" called "Attention-Deficit Hyperactivity Disorder" (ADHD) and includes it in the *DSM-III-R.*

❏ 1988—500,000 U.S. schoolchildren are diagnosed with ADHD, a new designer disease created with a vote of hands.

❏ 1990—U.S. Government welfare program offers low-income families annual payments of $450 cash for each "ADHD" child.

❏ 1991—Federal education grants given to local school programs began to add $400 annually for each child diagnosed with ADHD. The U.S. Department of Education formally recognized ADHD as a handicap and directed all state education officers to establish procedures to screen and identify ADHD children and provide them with special services.

❏ 1994—The APA releases the "new and improved" *Diagnostic and Statistical Manual of Mental Disorders—Fourth Edition (DSM-IV),* having more than tripled the number of mental disorders to 370 (compared to 112 in 1952).

❏ 1995—The percentage of children in U.S. welfare programs cited as having mental impairment including ADHD rose to 25 percent (from 5 percent in 1989).

❏ 1996—Physicians' practice surveys show 1.5 million children take antidepressants under their doctor's orders.[18]

❏ 1997—The number of American children labeled

with ADHD rose to 4.4 million (from 500,000 nine years earlier).

❑ 1998—An estimated four million children took the stimulant drug Ritalin or its equivalent (based on production/use quotas maintained by the U.S. Drug Enforcement Administration and national physician practice surveys).[19]

❑ 1999—The Colorado State School Board approved a resolution recommending that schools consider nonmedical solutions to behavior problems.[20]

❑ 2000—Approximately five million (as I mentioned earlier, I think the number is closer to seven million) American children are taking psychiatric drugs (including one or more of the following: Ritalin or some other stimulant, SSRI antidepressants and antipsychotic medications).[21]

❑ —The Texas Board of Education adopted a resolution recommending that schools consider nonmedical solutions to behavior problems.[22]

❑ 2001—IMS Health, a healthcare information company, reports that nearly twenty million prescriptions for Ritalin, Adderall and other stimulants were used to treat ADHD in 2000, a 35 percent increase over 1996.[23]

❑ —The Connecticut State Legislature unanimously passed and Gov. John G. Rowland signed the nation's first state law prohibiting teachers, counselors and other school officials from recommending psychiatric drugs for any child. The new law "reflects a growing backlash against what some see as overuse of Ritalin and other behavioral drugs." Legislation regarding psychiatric drugs in school has been proposed in nearly a dozen states.[24]

In his book *Prescription for Disaster: The Hidden Dangers in Your Medicine Cabinet*, Thomas Moore maintains that the wholesale prescribing of powerful drugs like Ritalin amounts to taking an "appalling risk" with our kids. He said the drugs were prescribed for "short-term control of behavior—not to reduce any identifiable hazard to [children's] health. Such large-scale chemical control of human behavior has not been previously undertaken in our society outside of nursing homes and mental institutions."[25]

While expanding its reach into society and dealing with a public backlash against its love affair with psychotropic drugs, psychiatry has done its best to shed a shady history. History indicates that psychiatry as a discipline is just as prone to the misuse and abuse of power as any other organized human endeavor.

FORCED STERILIZATION IN THE 1900s

For instance, the unthinkable happened when a psychiatrist named Edwin Katzen-Ellenbogen drafted a law in the early 1900s allowing the sterilization of epileptics, criminals and the incurably insane in New Jersey!

You may be thinking, *Surely the public and the media found such an idea shocking!* Actually, the law was passed, and twenty-two other American states followed New Jersey's lead. As for Dr. Katzen-Ellenbogen, he was later convicted of World War II war crimes.[26]

Meanwhile, the sterilization movement went worldwide. Sweden shortly followed suit in 1934, and by 1976, sixty thousand people were diagnosed as "genetically inferior" and sterilized, including teenage girls from poor families.[27] In Canada, psychiatrists claimed that two-thirds of mental illness was inherited and sterilization was the only feasible solution.[28] Over a five-decade period, sterilization of 4,728 people was authorized by the province of Alberta alone.[29] In 1998 and 1999, both Sweden and Alberta agreed to compensate survivors of involuntary sterilization.[30]

We must assume that only a tiny minority of psychiatrists today would approve of or participate in such heinous crimes against humanity. There are many conscientious mental health professionals who went into psychiatry, psychology and the behavioral sciences because they sincerely wanted to help people solve their problems and live happy lives.

These dedicated professionals are doing their best to find genuine solutions to the problems faced by children with the symptoms of ADD, ADHD and other disorders such as autism and PDD (pervasive development disorders). Many of them strongly disagree with some of the methods and guiding philosophies behind current treatments for these children.

THE INTENT—SUPPRESSION OF BEHAVIOR

Psychiatrist Peter Breggin, one of many mental health professionals who actively promote sensible, cautious and ethical care by psychiatrists and psychologists for their patients, testified on Capitol Hill:

> It is important for the Education Committee to understand that the ADD/ADHD diagnosis was developed specifically for the purpose of justifying the use of drugs to subdue the behaviors of children in the classroom. The content of the diagnosis in the 1994 *Diagnostic and Statistical Manual of Mental Disorders* of the American Psychiatric Association shows that it is specifically aimed at suppressing unwanted behaviors in the classroom.[31]

Perhaps we should not be surprised that many feel this is proof that psychiatry is applying overt control and restraint of human behavior. Is the scope of this growing faster than most people realize?

U.S. News & World Report columnist John Leo put it this way in a "Numbers a Shrink Can Love":

> According to *DSM-IV*, one problem alone—general anxiety disorder—will afflict 5 percent of the population, or 12 million people, at some point in their lifetime. "The pharmaceutical companies—the makers of Prozac, Xanax, and beta blockers for stage fright— love those numbers," say Kutchins and Kirk.[32]

And GAD is only one of the 374 official disorders that psychiatrists say hit half of all Americans.

> Worse, the psychiatrists are busy broadening definitions and lowering thresholds so that much of the other half will be listed as disordered too. *The clearest current example is attention deficit hyperactivity disorder, a label now being applied to many perfectly healthy small boys who bother school officials by misbehaving in class. ADHD cases have nearly doubled in five years.*
>
> ...New disorders do for psychiatrists what the litigation boom did for lawyers.[33]

DUBIOUS DRUG "TESTING" AT BEST

It is good to be able to joke about such an obvious mess, but sometimes the "treatment" for such disorders seems to come about as haphazardly as the allegedly make-believe disease.

Ray Woosley, chairman of pharmacology at Georgetown University Medical Center in Washington, D.C., made a frightening comment while discussing the need for caution when prescribing the SSRI family of antidepressants to children:

> We presume that children will respond the same as adults, but we don't know that. Physicians are having

to learn on the fly, and *every child is a new experiment.*[34]

Even worse, there are times when the potential for disaster or the horror of its reality just robs us of laughter. More and more evidence indicates there is a deadly side to subjecting the young to a liberal mixture of powerful medication, education, the "pill-a-day" philosophy of wellness and an overtly violent society.

The June 28, 1999 edition of *Insight on the News*, a magazine published by The Washington Times Corporation, featured the front cover headline, "Guns & Doses: The Common Link in the High-School Shootings May Be Psychotropic Drugs Like Ritalin."[35]

WERE THE SCHOOL SHOOTERS ON A PRESCRIBED HIGH?

Under a subhead that said, "...few Americans have noticed how many shooters were among the six million kids now on psychotropic drugs," author Kelly Patricia O'Meara listed five high-profile school shootings in which it is known or strongly suspected that the shooters had been prescribed psychotropic drugs.[36]

❑ A fifteen-year-old Idaho sophomore on Ritalin fired two shotgun rounds, narrowly missing students and school staff.

❑ Eric Harris, an eighteen-year-old senior at Columbine High School in Colorado, was under the influence of Luvox (fluvoxamine maleate), one of the new selective serotonin reuptake inhibitor, or SSRI, antidepressants, when he and Dylan Klebold killed a dozen students and a teacher before taking their own lives. Harris had been rejected by the Marine Corps just days before the shooting because he was taking the psychotropic drug.

❑ A fifteen-year-old boy in Conyers, Georgia, being treated for depression with a prescription for Ritalin started shooting and wounded six classmates.

❑ A fifteen-year-old boy in Springfield, Oregon, had been prescribed both Ritalin and Prozac. He murdered his parents and took his guns to school, killing two and wounding twenty-two.

❑ After a thirteen-year-old boy in Jonesboro, Arkansas, joined an eleven-year-old partner to open fire on his classmates, it was revealed he had been receiving psychiatric counseling. When asked about psychotropic drug therapy, his attorney would only say, "I think that is confidential information, and I don't want to reveal that."

O'Meara noted in her article that all of the shooters seemed to have something in common: "...all of the above were labeled as suffering from a mental illness and were being treated with psychotropic drugs that for years have been known to cause serious adverse effects when given to children."[37]

RESTORING SANITY WITH SANE METHODS

A noticeable rift has split the psychiatric community in recent years with a growing number of psychiatrists refusing to endorse the wholesale use of drugs to treat learning and behavior problems among the young. On the whole, these mental health doctors are doing their best to serve their patients while drawing on time-honored values of common sense, faith, intellectual and scientific integrity, and ethical standards of practice based on the physician's first rule—do no harm. We should applaud their efforts to restore sanity and mental well-being through sane methods.

Author Elliot S. Valenstein, Ph.D., closes this chapter with a summary observation and warning about the very real limits of neuropharmacology in the treatment of allegedly diseased brains:

> Contrary to what is claimed, no biochemical, anatomical, or functional signs have been found that reliably distinguish the brains of mental patients... [these] theories are held on to not only because there is nothing else to take their place, but also because they are useful in promoting drug treatment.
>
> *...all of the impressive knowledge of neuropharmacology has not really brought us closer to understanding the origin of mental disorders...* people with mental disorders may be encouraged when they are told that the prescribed drugs will do for them just what insulin does for a diabetic, but *the analogy is certainly not justified.*[38]

FIVE

The High/Low Jackpot: Sugar Levels and Learning Levels

O ne of America's most respected pediatricians, allergists and immunologists said, "If our automobiles put out blue smoke, jerked, jumped and got only six miles to the gallon, we'd check on the quality of the fuel we put in our cars' gas tanks. We certainly should do the same thing for our children."[1]

I'll never forget the mother who came to my office with her children several years ago for some training and educational materials. While she was talking to me, two of her children were busy bouncing off the walls. I believe that they might have done laps on my walls if I had let them. They were jumping up and down on the furniture, yelling, screaming and hitting each other.

The little girl who was sitting in my office with her mother decided to prop her feet up on my desk. I looked at her and said, "Could you take your feet off my desk? Thank you." The scene was so chaotic that I thought, *There's got to be something wrong with these youngsters' diet, unless there's an unbelievable discipline problem.* Yet, the mother seemed to be trying to discipline them. She had come to me because she felt so bad physically. Any parent knows it is especially difficult to discipline your kids when you don't feel well.

Finally I asked the mother, "Can I ask you a question? Do your children drink soft drinks?" Her answer was quick and short: "Well of course they drink soft drinks—all kids drink soft drinks." Sensing what was coming, I forged ahead.

"Excuse me," I said, "I don't mean to get you upset or anything, but do you mind telling me how many soft drinks per day each child drinks?"

"I don't know...three or four a day."

"Well that's 40 to 50 teaspoons of sugar a day that little five-year-old has put into his body, not to mention all the other foods that he eats every day. You might want to consider reducing their consumption of soft drinks and giving them water or something to drink other than sugar drinks."

That which I'd feared came upon me when she ended the conversation with a single blunt reply.

"Don't lecture me."

Finger pointing is for fools, but caring people feel compassion for those in pain or in need. I knew that this woman lashed out at me for a number of reasons. Most likely it was because she didn't feel well, and she also knew already that the diet she was providing for her children was inadequate at best and self-serving at worst.

THE AMERICAN TREND THAT LAUNCHED AN EPIDEMIC

Frankly, it often seems more convenient for overwhelmed parents to feed their kids the high-sugar, high-fat, low-nutrition fast foods that "everyone else eats." It has become the American way, a trend that helped launch an epidemic of physical and behavioral problems that threaten to sink our tottering educational system.

We are examining attention-deficit hyperactivity disorder in this book—what does a lady with out-of-control kids who drink too many soft drinks have to do with it?

It may have everything to do with the problem.

Two medical doctors, one an addiction specialist and the other a widely read medical expert who authored *The Ladies' Home Journal Medical Guide*, joined forces to write a highly acclaimed book on hidden addictions titled *The Hidden Addiction and How to Get Free*. The authors made an astounding statement that every parent of an allegedly ADHD or ADD child should consider:

> *Sugar addiction is the world's most widespread addiction,* and probably one of the hardest to kick. Because so many addictive parents share it, I believe it is the "basic addiction" that precedes all others. Most of my addicted patients tell me that at one time they craved sugar almost daily. Furthermore, few people recognize their sugar addiction.[2]

Let me make my point now and defend it in the pages that follow. If your child has been diagnosed or labeled as ADHD or ADD or tagged with some other learning disability or malady, check the fuel in his "gas tank" before you accept any diagnosis of mental deficiency or a prescription for stimulants or antidepressants.

MOST ADHD CHILDREN DRAMATICALLY HELPED BY DIETARY CHANGES

To quote Dr. William G. Crook, M.D., "There are many medical reports, including placebo-controlled, double-blind studies carried out in the 1990s, that show *most* children with ADHD can be helped significantly, even dramatically, *by dietary changes*."[3]

Refined sugar sensitivity remains a top suspect on my offender list for childhood behavior and learning problems. This seems logical in a nation where the average person consumes 160 pounds of sugar each year, but many medical professionals continue to scoff at the idea. It has been said that ignorance is bliss—in my practice I've learned that ignorance can be fatal.

We will look at an abbreviated list of sugar-sensitivity related symptoms in a moment, but first you should know something very few if any parents, psychiatrists, teachers or school meal planners seem to know. According to Ronald L. Hoffman, M.D.:

> Children appear to have a radically different response to sugar than adults. A recent study compared children's and adults' response to a sugar dose, measuring blood glucose and adrenaline every half-hour for five hours. Blood sugar levels remained in the normal range in both adults and children, but the adrenaline levels in the children were *ten times higher* than normal *up to five hours* after the sugar dose. The kids were experiencing a major hormonal wallop.[4]

That hormonal "wallop" is a natural part of the body's response when we eat sugar or "simple carbohydrates" such as refined white sugar, white flour, corn syrup and so forth. When these refined (or "nutritionally empty but metabolically dangerous") simple carbohydrates hit your system, they are converted into glucose and enter your bloodstream in a matter of minutes!

Your body's first response is to produce large amounts of insulin to process the glucose and reduce the sugar level in your bloodstream. Usually you "bottom out" with your blood sugar level dropping so low that you may feel the weakness, fatigue and spacey feeling so common to hypoglycemia. Again the body compensates, but this time it releases powerful natural stimulants from the adrenal glands—the most well-known of these hormones is the "fight or flight" hormone called adrenaline.

KIDS REACT TO SUGAR TEN TIMES MORE THAN ADULTS

As an adult, you know how you feel over a two-hour period if you eat nothing but a candy bar or ice cream. You know all about the roller-coaster ride of quick energy followed by an unnatural fatigue. That fatigue finally ends with a hormonal jolt that leaves you jittery and shaky for maybe an hour or so. Now multiply the high, the low and the jitters by a factor of ten—then imagine feeling that way for five hours instead of a half-hour! Congratulations; you've just taken an imaginary ride on America's favorite school-day roller coaster of sugar thrills, insulin spills and adrenaline shakes. It's enough to make anyone "act up" and stand up in class.

When a child eats pudding, ice cream or even mashed potatoes in the school lunchroom, the parade of horrors may begin at the same approximate moment that he finally takes his seat to start the afternoon classroom routine. (In most cases, he had probably just "run down" from the morning show after eating sugary breakfast foods or pancakes and syrup before beginning the school day.)

Dr. Hoffman wrote in 1997: "Recent medical opinion has strongly discounted the sugar connection." He went on to note that some studies suggest that while many kids seem to make the incredible sugar adjustment without measurable changes in their behavior, other children "who are susceptible to ADD or ADHD" have clearly adverse reactions to sugar.[5]

Let me remind you that terms such as "recent medical opinion" or "research indicates" should simply be seen as signals to dig deeper. "Recent medical opinion" is notorious for following "fads" and politically correct trends in vogue at the time. (See the Notes section for Dr. Hoffman's description of "The Inglefinger Effect," which explains the way new medications and procedures are accepted or rejected by the medical industry.[6])

WHY DO MOST DOCTORS DISMISS THE SUGAR FACTOR?

According to Dr. William G. Crook, most physicians remain skeptical toward the relationship of food allergies (including sugar) to brain dysfunction for two primary reasons:

❏ Other studies have concluded dietary change played little, if any, role in causing ADHD. (Some of these negative studies were funded by the Sugar Association and other food industries.)

❏ Most food sensitivities cannot be identified by the traditional allergy prick test.[7]

Dr. Crook concluded by noting since 1985, "double-blind, placebo-controlled studies published in the peer-reviewed literature provide documentation for the relationship of food allergies to ADHD."[8]

It has been my experience that virtually every child exhibits noticeable reactions to sugar and shows measurable improvements in behavior and learning rates when sugar is gradually removed from his or her diet. I suspect that many parents in North America would agree with my clinical observations. In one study, researchers found that 75 percent of the hyperactive children had abnormal results to glucose tolerance tests![9]

In his book *Help for the Hyperactive Child: A practical guide offering parents of ADHD children alternatives to Ritalin*, Dr. Cook says that he wrote the book specifically for family members and teachers of ADD children, especially those in four key categories. The fourth category includes those who "give a history of craving sugar and eating a nutritionally deficient diet."[10]

A "history of craving sugar" refers to people who feel they need sugar or refined flour products in every meal. Most of the time this craving for sugar produces clearly noticeable symptoms of a condition called hypoglycemia, a problem that affects approximately twenty million people in the United States.

YOUR JEKYLL AND HYDE MAY HAVE HYPOGLYCEMIA

Dr. Mary Ann Block, a nationally known osteopath, said, "Low blood sugar, or hypoglycemia, is *the most significant underlying problem I find in children who exhibit behavioral problems*. The symptoms of hypoglycemia are usually easy to identify. The child who is agitated or irritable when he or she wakes up in the morning or before meals and then is better after eating is probably affected by hypoglycemia. The child with the Jekyll and Hyde behavior, who is sweet and fine one minute and then for no apparent reason is agitated, angry and irritable the next, may have hypoglycemia."[11]

How can you tell that you or your child has hypoglycemia? Glance through the list of common hypoglycemic symptoms I have collected from patient interviews over many years of clinical nutritional work. Keep in mind that in most cases these symptoms disappear or lessen in severity when excess sugar and refined food products are avoided. They also lessen or disappear with better nutrition and improved lifestyle choices. The symptoms are pretty obvious in most cases.

- ❑ 67 percent of the hypoglycemics I interviewed suffer from exhaustion.
- ❑ 60 percent complain of chronic depression.
- ❑ 50 percent suffer from frequent insomnia.
- ❑ 50 percent said they battle frequent feelings of anxiety.

Other symptoms commonly reported include irritability, headaches, sweating, inner trembling, muscle pain and backache, crying spells, phobias, difficulty in concentration, numbness, chronic indigestion, mental confusion, cold hands or feet, blurred vision, muscular twitching or cramps, joint pain, antisocial behavior, restlessness, obesity, staggering, abdominal spasms, fainting or blackouts, convulsions, suicidal tendencies, forgetfulness, nervousness, constant worrying, ravenous hunger between meals, indecisiveness, a decrease in or a total absence of sex drive (in both females and males), craving for sweets, impotence in males, moodiness, allergies, feelings of going crazy, lack of coordination, itching and crawling sensations on the skin, gasping for breath, smothering smells, sighing and yawning, unconsciousness, night terrors, nightmares, dry or burning mouth, ringing in the ears, peculiar breath or perspiration odor, temper tantrums, hot flashes and noise and light sensitivity.

THE BODY REGULATES SUGAR LEVELS WITH HORMONES

I realize these symptoms are extremely broad in scope and general in nature, but that simply underscores how difficult and pervasive hypoglycemia can be. The symptoms are broad because the human body regulates blood sugar levels through the hormonal system, and hormones have a tremendous effect on the way we feel from minute to minute.

We've already considered the way adrenaline affects the human body when it is released into the bloodstream to counteract low blood sugar. Nevertheless, Dr. Block's comments on the effect of epinephrine, or adrenaline as it's commonly known, are worth repeating:

> When adrenaline is dumped into a child's bloodstream, the child feels the fight-or-flight energy surge, reacting to the way the chemical makes him feel. Even if he is sitting comfortably in the classroom, trying to pay attention, an adrenaline release will have a profound

effect. The pupils in the eyes dilate, the heart rate increases, and he cannot sit still. He cannot concentrate and can become agitated.

Any little thing will now trigger him to act aggressively, even angrily. Such behavior is not conscious; the child does not choose to act that way. It is a physiological reaction. How uncomfortable and confusing to the mind and body to have to deal with common, day-to-day issues as if they were major, cataclysmic events. Yet adrenaline release occurs out of a natural protective mechanism, activated not by danger or fear but by other factors: what we eat or don't eat.[12]

Remember that this incredibly uncomfortable cycle begins when sugar-rich foods enter the system of a child or adolescent. It is the body's frantic effort to counteract the explosive influx of sugar into the bloodstream with insulin that dramatically lowers blood sugar and, in turn, triggers the emergency adrenaline rush.

The good news is that all of this is avoidable. No, you don't have to totally eliminate sugar from the diet, but you should do whatever it takes to remove your child or yourself from harm's way. Sugar addiction and hypoglycemia can literally ruin your life. At the very least, they limit personal performance in the classroom, at home and in the workplace.

UNCHECKED HYPOGLYCEMIA AND DIABETES

Perhaps the most frightening fact about hypoglycemia is that if it continues unchecked, in many cases it may lead to the opposite extreme of the blood sugar disorders: diabetes. Diabetes is far more severe than hypoglycemia. If it isn't controlled, it can cause blindness, loss of limbs and even fatal heart disease. Diabetes is the third-worst killer in America, claiming more than three hundred thousand lives per year.

What does diabetes have to do with children diagnosed with ADHD or ADD? As we've already seen, many respected medical professionals believe ADHD is a misdiagnosis, a prime example of health providers overlooking the cause of disease for the sake of more convenient "treatment" of outward symptoms.

When hypoglycemia in an adult or child goes undetected and untreated, it will frequently degenerate into fully developed diabetes. Would you want your child to suffer from hypoglycemia needlessly while taking a Class II restricted drug like Ritalin or Adderall to mask the symptoms of a potentially deadly (and completely preventable) disease?

There is a better way to live, and there are better ways to help children with learning or behavioral problems. It just may not be as easy as popping a psychotropic pill in their mouths each day, but why worry about "easiness" or comfort when you have a chance to give your children normal lives? Most parents I know will do anything to help their children face a future free of drug-induced side effects, health complications, mental aberrations, social stigma and an increased potential for drug addictions. If you've read this far, you must share their convictions. To learn more about proper eating and balancing your body's sugar levels, call my office at 1-800-726-1834 and order a copy of my *Eat, Drink & Be Healthy!* program.

SIX

Your Child in a "Dumbed-Down" World

T he following statement wasn't issued by a shadowy fringe group or by conspiracy theorists. It came from the National Commission on Excellence in Education's April 1983 report on American education, titled "A Nation at Risk."[1]

> If an unfriendly foreign power had attempted to impose on America the mediocre education system we have today, it would have well been viewed as an act of war. As it stands, we have done this to ourselves.

Thirteen years later, a National Adult Literacy Survey confirmed many of our worst fears. As many as ninety-four million American adults held such poor literacy skills that they could barely function in society or the workplace![2]

What has happened to us? In the words of Job, "The thing I greatly feared has come upon me, and what I dreaded has happened to me" (Job 3:25). Today, we clearly live in a "dumbed-down" nation.

An estimated four million American children enter the first grade each year expecting to learn how to read, and their parents assume the public school system will produce the same results it obtained in previous generations. Education officials and teachers' union spokespersons may claim success, but many an average school child seems incapable of reading those claims in a newspaper article! Parents across the United States suspect that something has gone terribly wrong.

Are children of this era less intelligent than children of the 1930s and 1940s? Absolutely not! Have America's children fallen victim to some epidemic that leaves large numbers of them learning impaired? Many experts would shout, "Absolutely!" The hard statistics seem to confirm their darkest suspicions.

❏ Despite unprecedented investments in education facilities, training and teacher salaries over the last decade, the nation's average SAT scores have dropped almost eighty points![3]

❏ The National Center for Education Statistics announced in 1997 that *40 percent* of America's workforce (age sixteen and over) lack the [literacy or reading] *skills* needed in "managerial, technical, high-level sales, skilled clerical or craft and precision production occupations."[4]

❏ The United States had a higher concentration of adults in the lowest literacy level than nearly all the other countries surveyed in an international study of adult literacy![5]

Noting that the *illiteracy rate* for urban African American children in 1990 was around *40 or 50 percent*, up from *only 9.2 percent* in 1930, one noted reading advocate asked, "How is it that sixty years ago, without Head Start, without Title One compensatory education, without integration, black children learned so much better than they do today?"[6] One doesn't need an advanced degree in education or rocket science to realize something is wrong with our educational system.

I have thoroughly researched the subject as a concerned parent, as a former college instructor and as a health services provider seeking answers for ADD and ADHD patients and their parents. What I've discovered may surprise you.

The "dumbing down" of America's schools didn't happen overnight. It was a gradual process that appears to be directly related to a gradual shift away from the proven foundations of individual literacy, biblical concepts of right and wrong behavior and measurable educational goals and personal achievement. If the writings of leading educational thinkers before and after the turn of the previous century account for anything, it seems this gradual shift was no accident.

"LEARNING TO READ EARLY...IS A PERVERSION"

John Dewey, clearly the leading philosopher of the so-called "progressive" education movement, wrote an essay titled "The Primary-Education Fetich" in 1898, in which he chided the educators for focusing on the instruction of reading. He said:

> There is...a false educational god whose idolaters are legion, and whose cult influences the entire educational system. This is language study—the study not of foreign language, but of English; not in higher, but in primary education. It is almost an unquestioned assumption, of educational theory and practice both, that the first three years of a child's school-life shall be mainly taken up with learning to read and write in his own language. If we add to this the learning of a certain amount of numerical combinations, we have the pivot about which primary education swings...
>
> My proposition is, that conditions—social, industrial, and intellectual—have undergone such a radical

change, that the time has come for a thoroughgoing examination...

The plea for the predominance of *learning to read in early school life because of the great importance attaching to literature seems to me a perversion.*[7]

Dewey believed teachers should use the latest "scientific findings" of psychology (especially the findings of Russian physiologist Ivan Pavlov on "conditioned response" in animals) to develop "proper social attitudes" in children rather than the basic literacy skills of reading, writing and arithmetic. He proposed this change could take place "over several generations" of children.

OPPOSITION TO JUDEO-CHRISTIAN PRINCIPLES

This new breed of educators led by Dewey in the mid-1800s and early 1900s was part of an academic elite determined to shape the world according to a new order conspicuously opposed to anything resembling Judeo-Christian principles from the Scriptures.

[The "progressives" had essentially] rejected the religion of their fathers. They rejected the Bible and put their new faith in science, evolution and psychology. Science provided the means to know the material world. Evolution explained the origin of man, thus relegating the story of Genesis to mythology, and psychology institutionalized the scientific study of human nature and provided *the scientific means to control human behavior.*[8]

What does this have to do with ADHD, ADD and with helping your child excel in school? More than you might believe. For better or for worse, what happens in university educational departments today tends to filter down to

America's classrooms in one way or another. The departure from proven biblical and moral foundations in the mid-1800s began to severely affect the nation's classrooms in the 1960s as "progressive education principles" began to dominate every level of the public school systems.

At my request, Jeanie Eller, one of the nation's leading literacy experts according to The National Right to Read Foundation, granted me an interview specifically for this chapter.[9] Over the last thirty-six years, Jeanie has taught people of all ages how to read. Additionally, she has gathered extensive information about teaching students diagnosed with ADD and ADHD.

Eller traces many of the nation's literacy problems back to the "reforms" of key education leaders around the turn of the century such as John Dewey, James McKeen Cattell, Edward L. Thorndike and Edmund Burke Huey. Recalling John Dewey's strategy to affect the change "over several generations" of children, Eller says, "Guess what? We're there."

The "progressives" felt elementary students were being taught to read far too early and with methods that were "unscientific." The "whole word" theory of reading was developed from supposed scientific ideas drawn from early psychological theories. Its modern relative, the "look-say" method, is a rigid fixture in the "Outcomes-Based Education" (OBE) model incorporated in the "Goals 2000" education program passed under former President Bill Clinton.

TEACHING READING TODAY

Teachers use four methods to teach American students how to read, according to Eller. The *whole language philosophy* believes children will learn to read on their own naturally. The movement operates on the premise that learning to read is like talking or walking. Children will learn to read when they are ready, and teachers are simply facilitators who read stories. The children memorize the contents, then "magically" figure out how to read on their own, in their own timing and using their own energy.

Under this method, if the parent goes to the teacher and asks, "Why isn't my fourth grader reading?", the instructor of this method may respond, "He must not be ready to read. He'll learn when he is ready." The answer remains the same, even if the child is in the eighth grade. "He may not be ready."

The whole language method refers to incorrect spelling as "creative spelling" and maintains that children "magically" learn how to spell as well. Eller said 85 percent of U.S. schools use the whole language method.

Sight-reading is another popular method, one character-ized by the old "Dick and Jane" readers. Teachers typically use flash cards or require students to memorize lists of words. The goal is to have children *memorize more than a million words* over an eight-year period in a basal reading system. "It's absolute nonsense," Eller said. Many adults have a fond attachment to the Dick and Jane readers, but most of them actually learned how to read through phonics *before* they were introduced to the readers. By that point, they were "immune" to the confusion and limitations that sight-reading techniques usually produce in young readers.

PLUMMETING READING SCORES— IT'S NO ACCIDENT

The third method is the *phonetic approach*. Unfortunately, only 15 percent of America's schools use phonetics or any type of phonics. The percentage of schools using the phonics method continually dropped due to the concerted efforts of the educators influenced by the "progressive" leaders over the last one hundred years. It is no accident that the reading scores have plummeted to such a degree that fourth graders can't read a fourth-grade book or read the average newspaper. Parents are beginning to demand that schools use proven reading methods, which are based on current research (or *phonics*).

Teachers using the phonics method teach students the alphabet code of the English language. The Phoenicians invented the alphabetic code system five thousand years ago, and this method worked for multiple languages and cultures throughout the ages. It produced some of America's greatest literary geniuses until the U.S. schools began to change to sight-reading and whole language.

The fourth method used to teach reading blends together all three teaching methods into an *eclectic method*. "This system uses a little of this and a little of that, which is the least effective means to teach children to read," Eller said. "Unfortunately, many teachers feel this method is a 'balanced' approach instead of giving children the code of the English language in first grade—which the research validates as the best method." The early mastery of the alphabetic code was once so crucial to independent growth and study that thirty or forty years ago, students in the first grade weren't allowed to advance until they learned to read. Teachers knew that reading was the most important learning block for future study.

The first sight-reading books, also known as "Dick and Jane" books, were published in 1932. By the late 1950s, they were in every school. Sight-reading books are based on the premise that two hundred words are central to any type of reading—whether a magazine or an academic book. These "high frequency words" appear 70 percent of the time. Therefore, the method's creators reasoned, *If we have children memorize these two hundred words by sight, then we can speed up the teaching and reading.*

"The idea is absolute nonsense," said Eller, "because you only have to learn 70 *phonograms* in order to be able to read. The book companies loved it, though, because they could spread out the teaching of reading over eight years. They began to sell textbooks to the schools as though reading was a subject. Reading is not a subject; it is a skill that you learn once and use for the rest of your life."

By the late 1950s or early 1960s, every school in America was using these basal readers with the sight method "Dick and Jane" books. Even though the textbooks had changed, the schools were full of wonderful teachers *who knew the phonetic code* and continued to supplement the teaching so children could learn how to sound out the words. The problems associated with the switch from phonics to whole language didn't become evident until these teachers began to retire.

The new generation of young instructors genuinely loved children and worked hard, but they didn't have this supplemental information to teach the children to read. This period marked the beginning of "remedial reading" and "special education," terms that are now commonplace in the nation's educational system. A few years later, the move toward special educational programs had evolved to include "learning disabilities," ADD, dyslexia, hyperactivity and other labels.

The whole language movement began in the early 1970s and spread throughout the public schools through extensive promotion from teacher colleges. Education professors started the whole language method as a theory-driven experiment on our children. Since the method generally fails to teach students how to read, it requires teachers to watch for mistakes conveniently called "miscues." Under this system, if a child looks at a horse and calls it a pony, that is a "good miscue" because "he's getting the concept."

The whole language method also assumes that a child will learn to spell by reading. Eller said, "Recently I posed this question to the father of whole language, Kenneth Goodman: 'How can a child learn to spell if you say it's OK for them to look at a horse and say the word *pony*? Are they going to spell pony h-o-r-s-e?'"

GROUNDBREAKING NEW RESEARCH

Eller says new research from the National Institute of Child Health and Human Development, from Harvard University and from the United States Department of Education contends the nation's schools must begin teaching "intensive, systematic, directive instruction in phonics in first grade."

Despite these studies from three major research organizations, the whole language method continues to be widely used across America. According to Eller, "The whole language experts are saying our program works, but you didn't give us enough money or time."

Noting that every state in the nation allocates at least 50 percent of its annual budget to education, yet the schools still can't teach the children to read, Eller said, "I think they should cut down on this funding, and it will force them to find reading methods that work."

More than ninety million adults in the U.S. (over half of the population) are functionally illiterate—they can't fill out a job application or look for the name of a product on a grocery store shelf. They must look for a picture. It is for this reason that public restrooms have pictographs to distinguish the men's room from the ladies' room. "These adults who can't read came right through the public school system," Eller said.

If you consider all of the countries that track their literacy rate, the United States ranks forty-ninth—which means that a number of Third World countries are ahead of America. In 1974, when Eller began to do her research on literacy levels, the United States ranked thirteenth. In twenty-five years we've dropped rapidly to an even lower rank.

PERCEPTION VS. EFFECTIVE EDUCATION?

"At the time of the 'Nation at Risk' report in 1983, the difficulties could have been fixed," Eller said. "The discipline and the literacy rate weren't too far out of hand. But instead of fixing it, the teachers' union said, 'Oh my, we have to change the public's *perception* of education.'"

Rather than fix the root problems, educational leaders pumped money into an intensive national public relations campaign that was extremely successful. (That was when bumper stickers appeared proclaiming, "My child is an honor student at John Doe School.") As a result, vast amounts of federal funds were allocated to perpetuate and enlarge a failed system with no true reforms.

If the figures that shook the nation's confidence in the 1983 "Nation at Risk" report and the figures from the more recent National Adult Literacy Survey point to a failing educational system, then what is the answer? Not everyone can afford a private school, and homeschooling simply isn't an option for everyone.

IS THE SYSTEM THE CULPRIT?

Parents often discover that if they ever complain about their child's inability to read, some educators will quickly pin the blame on the child. In some cases, they may even suggest that a child struggling to read has ADD or is hyperactive. If you encounter this attitude, be sure to ask, "What system are you using to teach my child to read?" You may well discover that the teaching methodology itself is part of the problem.

Samuel L. Blumenfeld, noted author and editor of *The Blumenfeld Education Letter*, reviewed a book about ADHD by two medical doctors and noted that virtually every ADD case history described by the authors *involved some traumatic experience in early education.* He said, "Apparently, none of the experts on ADD has bothered to investigate the possible *school causes* of attention deficit disorder..."[10]

Many children develop learning problems during the first few years of formal education. When I mentioned some of the problems to Jeanie Eller, she said, "I've seen many children in the classroom who have been labeled with attention deficit disorder, hyperactivity, dyslexia and dysphonia. I've seen all of the labels that they can put on these little guys. While these children may have some symptoms, I've never met a person who is truly dyslexic. Some of these children were hyperactive, but when you look at the broad criteria for ADD, all kids fall somewhere in those categories of being either slow or fast, quiet or noisy."

CORRECT THE DAMAGE?

The first step toward success is to make your child's education a personal priority. Invest the time and energy to understand how children learn to read. I am convinced that the time-tested method of phonics is a necessary part of a maximum solution for teaching hyperactive students.

Ironically, phonics was the teaching method most hated by the "progressive educators" led by John Dewey. Their first order of business was to replace phonics with a newer, "more scientific" method of teaching reading based on emerging psychological theories. An early attempt to adopt these "scientific" methods in Boston ended in wholesale failure and virtual rebellion by Boston teachers who demanded a return to tried and true phonics methods.[11]

The real irony was that these "progressive" thinkers actually *regressed* from the highly advanced alphabet-based system of writing developed by the Phoenicians around 2000 B.C.

Before the invention of the alphabet, people and civilizations such as the ancient Egyptians used "pictographs," or graphic symbols, that looked like the things they represented. You can see a modern version of pictographs on every public restroom door in America. Pictographs evolved into "ideographs," which were symbols that represented things that could not be "pictured," such as good and evil or never and forever.

The Chinese written language is an ideographic system—every character represents a thing, a word or an idea, and there is no alphabet. One scholar wrote of the Chinese written language:

> ...there really is no end to the language; it is infinite. Some writers have estimated the number of words [hence, characters] as high as two hundred and sixty thousand, eight hundred and ninety-nine (Montucci); but the total of really different symbols in use among good writers will not exceed twenty-five thousand. Ten thousand signs, however, will enable one to read any book; while three thousand is sufficient for all ordinary purposes.[12]

In the Western hemisphere, everything changed when someone discovered that all human languages are spoken using a small number of similar sounds and devised symbols to represent those basic sounds. All a student must do to read a book in English is learn to recognize *only twenty-six letters* of the alphabet and the sounds they represent. Then he must be drilled in consonant-vowel combinations (such as ba, ca and da) until recognition is automatic. The memorization of a million English words over an eight-year timespan as required by the *sight-reading method* is a giant step backward in Eller's view.

THEY COULD READ ANYTHING!

Jeanie Eller once led a class of illiterate adults from total illiteracy to literacy *in just two weeks* using the proven phonics method, and she did it in front of Oprah Winfrey's national television audience! "I taught these adults exactly as I teach children," Eller said. "We started with sounds, then we learned how these sounds make words and then sentences. Each step of the way, I used decodable text—which means I never gave them a sentence with a long vowel sound until I taught them long vowels.

"We covered the seventy phonograms of English. *When they finished, they could read anything in English.* The oldest person in the group was a sixty-nine-year-old man who desperately wanted to read his Bible. At the end of the two-week course, he could. Once a reader masters this simple 'code,' he or she can literally sound out any and all unfamiliar English words with great accuracy."

> The beauty of the alphabet is that it permitted the writer to convey his thoughts with precision and accuracy because the written words were a *direct representation of a spoken language.* This was not the case with ideographs which represented ideas that could be expressed in many different ways...
>
> The advantages of alphabetic writing were immediately understood by the ancients...The new alphabetic writing system replaced all of the ideographic systems being used in the West and became the greatest boon to intellectual and spiritual advancement that civilization has ever known. It was so simple that even children could learn to read.[13]

THE HIGHEST LITERACY IN HISTORY

The Romans systematically taught their children how to read using phonics. "This was the method used throughout the Western world to achieve the highest literacy of any civilization in history, and this is the method which is now virtually banned in the government schools of the English-speaking world."[14]

G. Stanley Hall, a leading progressive and mentor for John Dewey and others, wrote:

> The best pedagogues are now drifting surely, if slowly, toward the conclusion that instead of taking half the

time of the first year or two of school to teach reading, little attention should be paid to it before the beginning of the third year, that nature study, language work, and other things should take the great time and energy now given to this subject.[15]

In contrast, Eller claims that according to the latest research studies, the skill of reading should be taught *and finished* by the end of first grade or at least by second grade. In second grade, the child should be able to fluently read the newspaper. Noting that another set of statistics from the National Association of Progress Tests show two-thirds of high school students can't read high school material, Eller said, "To me, that amounts to criminal negligence. You make a student sit in school every day for ten or eleven years, yet they are not given the basic skills."

When students aren't taught the rudimentary elements of education, they can't do their schoolwork. Yet, they are forced to sit in the classroom. It's no wonder that they become troublemakers and discipline problems—from boredom if nothing else!

GRADUATING WITH A DIPLOMA THEY CAN'T READ

According to Eller, 85 percent of the schools in America use teaching methods that do not teach children to read in first and second grade. Perhaps we can better understand why so many children seem to graduate from high school and receive a diploma they are apparently *unable to read.*

"If I get them in first grade, they don't develop the symptoms of ADD," Eller said. "Nor will they be labeled as 'learning disabled' and funneled into special education." Yet the reading instruction must meet several criteria:

❑ It must be based in phonetics.

❏ It must be taught in a logical, sequential progression.

❏ It must be based on direction instruction.

A number of elements must be accomplished precisely for the child to successfully learn to read. The first step is *phonemic awareness*. This is when a child is taught that words are made from sounds.

Many parents naturally help their children develop phonemic awareness by playing rhyming games and singing nursery rhymes. It helps to emphasize the various syllables in each word.

Jeanie said her little granddaughter told her, "I want baby food," and she answered, "I don't have any baby food." Evidently the toddler thought she had been misunderstood, so she repeated her request. But the second time she said, "I want *ba-by* food." The fact that she broke down the word into syllables and clearly enunciated them showed the first signs of phonemic awareness.

The child moves into phonics in the second step and learns to connect sounds with the appropriate letters from the alphabet. There are twenty-six letters in the English alphabet, and we use forty-four sounds to make more than a million words. We arrange these sounds in different order to make words. There are seventy different ways to write these sounds.

TEACH CHILDREN THE "CODE" EARLY

"Once you have the phonic code, immediately you can read every word that you speak and understand, and then you can begin learning new things," Eller said. "If you teach the children this 'code' at an early age, they may never exhibit the symptoms of hyperactivity."

There are two overlooked problems that often mimic the generalized symptoms of hyperactivity. Many children labeled hyperactive are actually bored, and others were never trained to read from left to right. If they were trained in any of the "whole language" methods, they were taught to look at the pictures and jump to the end of the line to "guess" the words they don't recognize.

The frenetic eye movements produced by this reading method appear to create the chaotic disorganization and poor-attention focus symptoms of ADD or ADHD. Many teachers believe that an ADD or hyperactive child will do well on a computer, and they attribute the improvement to a particular computer software program that has a reputation for excellence. "It's not the program," Eller said. "The computer forces them to read from left to right—it's automatically built into the system."

Eller said that if you give children the "code" of the English language through a phonetic teaching method, you create early readers and lifelong readers who love to read.

THE ROLE OF DIET

In my own research, I've found that diet, discipline and other types of behavioral and environmental stimuli have a profound affect on hyperactive children and their ability to learn and read phonetically. When I mentioned this to Eller, she said, "Diet plays a huge role in the entire makeup of the child. If the student comes to school without breakfast or after consuming a chemical drug like Ritalin, they are certainly not going to be able to achieve as well as a child who has a nourishing breakfast."

Even in this case, Jeanie Eller doesn't distinguish between the hyperactive child and the normal student. However, she does insist that older children with reading problems need to begin at the beginning. In most cases, these youngsters were not taught how to read phonetically.

Ms. Eller conducted a summer reading camp in Colorado during which she taught students how to read in just *two weeks.* She remembers one fifth-grader who couldn't read and was labeled as dyslexic, hyperactive, ADD and was considered a consistent troublemaker. Eller said, "Based on tests run by 'experts' at one state university, his mother was told the boy was dyslexic and probably would never be able to read or write."

He wore his hair down over his eyes like a shaggy dog, making visual contact virtually impossible. Eller began to teach about the alphabetic code and said, "I could see the light bulb begin to turn on for him. He suddenly understood how words were made. When we put the letters with the sounds, the boy couldn't keep the hair out of his eyes. His face was exuberant, and he began participating."

By the third morning of the camp, the boy entered the room with his mother—and a short haircut. He had told his mother, "Take me to the barbershop. I have to get this hair out of my eyes." She could not believe the transformation in her child. She had fought constantly with him over his hair and appearance. At the end of the two-week camp, he could read anything, and he could write and spell as well.

"I PREFER THE HYPERACTIVE STUDENT"

Eller has also had great success teaching children who were taking Ritalin. "They are like little zombies when they enter my class," she said. "I prefer the hyperactive student because I use an extremely active, multisensory program in which we sing songs, play games and alternate between standing and sitting. If you enter my classroom, you can't point out the students labeled as 'hyperactive' because every one of the students is active—yet it is *controlled learning*. The learning is accomplished in drill and rhyme and song format, which the students love, and it motivates them to learn to read!

"After using these techniques for thirty-six years," Eller says, "I've never met a student whom I felt should be on the medication." (She counsels concerned parents to only consider recommendations for medication for ADHD as a *last resort*, after they have provided their children with an *intensive phonics program* so they can function in school and *a good healthy diet*.)

ILLITERACY AND DELINQUENCY

Albert Shanker of the American Federation of Teachers said, "If children do not learn to read by the fourth grade, it is not likely that they will learn to read." Eller believes that many of the behavioral and academic problems experienced in the public schools stem from an early failure to read. It balloons into larger problems of boredom, frustration, damaged self-esteem and anger.

Eller's theory is supported by a major government study that revealed that *80 percent* of the students who appear in juvenile court are illiterate. Michael Bruner conducted a major research study for the Office of Juvenile Justice in Washington, D.C. He hoped to discover the root problem for juvenile violence and the tendency toward juvenile gangs.

The study crossed into every ethnic and socioeconomic group in America, examining rural America and suburbia and looking at families with high, middle and low incomes. Combine Bruner's 80 percent illiteracy rate for the "entry level" appearance before juvenile courts with the fact that *85 percent* of the people in prison are illiterate as well. Again, this statistic has nothing to do with the particular ethnic or social-economic classes of the prison population. The problem was at least partially rooted in the individuals' inability to read.

"If you teach children to read in the first grade so they can be good students and learn something," Eller said, "then they can get jobs when they finish school. I'm enough of a realist to know that literacy won't solve all of society's ills, but I am also convinced you would see many of our social problems begin to diminish with higher literacy among our children. Right now, we have children who have been through twelve or thirteen years of school who can't even fill out a job application! This is a potential social time bomb just waiting to explode."

THE HOMESCHOOLING ALTERNATIVE

In the early days of America, there were no organized public schools. American children learned to read in the home, and their parents taught them morals and ethics at the same time. The first step in homeschooling was and still is to learn how to read, then students may advance through other topics. (Eller favors such an approach.)

Homeschooled children always score the highest in national reading tests according to Eller. Private-schooled children rank next, and public school children rank the lowest. (Few people realize that nationwide, 50 percent of public schoolteachers have their own children in *private* schools.) The average homeschooler in seventh grade who takes a standardized test will score at the same level as a twelfth grader in the public school. "The reason for the difference with the homeschooler is simple," Eller said. "The homeschool parent teaches the child to read first, then he or she studies the subject matter. Of course, they are going to prefer something that works."

FORCED TO PRODUCE RESULTS

Some people are going to be reading these words and say, "Wait a minute. There's a reason the public schools are last: They have to accept everybody, and that's why they can't do a good job."

"That's not the reason that the private schools rank higher," Jeanie Eller contends. "It's because the private schools have to produce results. If you pay to send your child to a private school while you also pay taxes to support your local public school system, you will hold that private school to very high standards. If the school doesn't teach your child to read, you won't even think about sending your child back there for another year." This forces private schools to be results-oriented and to remain keenly aware of the competition."

Unfortunately, public schools are not required to produce results nor are they held accountable. "It seems the public schools can destroy children's lives with impunity," Eller said. "The teachers are certainly not the bad guys and the children are not stupid. The parents are not evil either. *The problem is the method.* Yet very few will dare to question it."

Some of the schools in the Montgomery, Alabama, school district were placed on academic alert after reading scores of students dropped to the lowest tenth percentile of all readers. The state was threatening to take over the schools. Therefore, the school district began to use the Action Reading Program, the phonics-based reading program taught by Jeanie Eller and many other reading experts.[16]

The Montgomery students moved from the bottom of the reading bracket up to the eightieth and ninetieth percentile—*in just one year!* When teachers have the right information, they can teach their students to read. When students master the skills of reading, we unshackle their future and release them to learn independently for the rest of their lives.

CAN ANYONE LEARN TO READ?

"If a person can see, hear and carry on a normal conversation, he or she can learn to read," according to Eller. One day she was taking listener calls on a live radio show when a mother called in to say, "My son has dysphonia."

Eller responded, "I've never heard of that. What is it?"

"The teacher says he cannot hear sounds, and as a result, he can never learn to read with phonics."

"Oh, I'm sorry your son is deaf," Jeanie said.

This mother sounded perturbed. "I didn't say he was deaf. I said he couldn't hear sounds."

Eller said, "Wait a minute...can he talk?"

"Yes."

"And how old is he?"

"Thirteen."

Jeanie asked, "How did he learn to talk if he can't hear sounds?"

She said, "I've never thought about that."

"Does he ever listen to the radio?"

"Yes, he loves to listen to the radio. He even sings along because he knows the words to every song."

Eller asked, "How can he listen and repeat and learn music if he can't hear sounds? If the child can see, hear and talk, then there is absolutely no excuse for that child not learning to read."

The same statement holds true for students labeled as ADD, ADHD and other learning-disabled terms. If you want to help your child excel in a "dumbed-down world," then give him or her a gift that keeps on giving. Make sure he or she learns how to read by mastering the phonetic code of the English language. When you do, the virtually unlimited knowledge banks of literature, language and libraries will be his or hers for the reading. (You can order Jeanie Eller's excellent reading program by calling my office at 800-726-1834.)

SEVEN

Autism—the New Wave

As many as one in every three hundred American children fell victim to a mysterious disorder called "autism" last year that few doctors knew about just fifty years ago.[1]

More than one-half million Americans have been diagnosed with autism or some form of pervasive developmental disorder (PDD), making it one of the most common developmental disabilities in the nation. It strikes four times as many boys as it does girls, and it crosses all lines of race, ethnicity, social standing, lifestyle and educational levels.[2]

Dr. Michael J. Goldberg put it this way: "While training as a pediatrician, I was told if I saw one autistic child in a lifetime of practice it would be one too many. What I am seeing today is not the autism I learned about in medical school twenty years ago. What was once a relatively rare disorder is now twenty times more likely to occur."[3]

There are differences between "classic autism"—which occurs in only one or two infants per ten thousand births—and the epidemic of new "autistic syndrome" cases that occur in one out of every five hundred children (rates as high as one to two hundred fifty have been suggested) according to Dr. Goldberg.

Parents generally notice that something is wrong in infants with classic autism in the first three to six months of life. Autistic syndrome symptoms, however, generally show up after young children develop normal speech and motor skills, show affection and demonstrate above-average intelligence.

Autism and autism syndrome conditions are still diagnosed according to American Psychiatric Association guidelines listed in the *DSM-IV*, but Dr. Goldberg says that autism, particularly autistic syndrome, is now considered a medical condition rather than a psychiatric or mental disorder. He believes that a majority if not all cases of autistic syndrome are "immune mediated" (related to dysfunction in the immune or autoimmune system) and are open to medical and nutritional therapy.[4]

Ironically, many medical and governmental sources downplay the apparent surge of new autism cases by attributing them to "expanded" definitions of autism. Dr. Sam Katz, a pediatrician and professor at Duke University, told Ed Bradley in a *60 Minutes* television documentary program: "A child who was called 'autistic' in 1971 is only one of a group who would now be called 'autistic' in 1999 or 2000. The diagnosis has been greatly broadened." When asked if there has been an epidemic of autism, he said, "I would hesitate to describe anything as an epidemic of autism."[5]

AUTISM—#1 DISABILITY IN CALIFORNIA

Figures released by California's Department of Developmental Services (DDS) at this writing have apparently removed all doubt that we are facing a full-scale epidemic. California's DDS announced that autism is now the number one disability entering its developmental services system!

Autism was once thought to be a rare disorder caused by a "refrigerator mother," and more recently it was thought to be a rare genetic disease. Now, it is classified as the number one disability entering California's developmental services system at an alarming and accelerated rate, surpassing mental retardation, cerebral palsy, epilepsy and all other conditions similar to mental retardation.

Prior to the epidemic, autism had historically accounted for 3 percent of individuals taken into California's developmental services system. Today, according to the California Department of Developmental Services, not including PDD, NOS, Asperger's or any other autistic spectrum disorder, *autism accounts for an amazing 37 percent of new intakes.*[6]

The statistics are staggering. California processed 664 new students who were diagnosed with autism and eligible for special services in just one three-month period! This was a 27 percent increase over the same period last year, amounting to an influx of seven "fully autistic" children every day, seven days a week.

California's overburdened public school system absorbed more children with "level one autism" in the first half of 2001 than in any other year from 1969 through 1998! At this rate, California's schools will add more than 2,700 additional autistic students to the rolls in this year alone. That is equal to all of the new cases of autism reported in thirteen and one-half years prior to the 1979–1980 school year. It exceeds the total number of autistic students entering the system in all of 1994, 1995 and 1996 combined.[7]

A 556 PERCENT INCREASE!

A researcher and branch chief for the U.S. Centers for Disease Control and Prevention (CDC) told a U.S. congressional committee that the number of U.S. children with autism who received special education services increased 556 percent from 1991 through 1997! She described the economic ramifications of the problem as follows:

Local, state and federal education departments spent approximately $49.2 billion in the 1998–99 school year on special education programs for children with developmental disabilities. The cost of special education for a child with autism is often more than $30,000 per year to the family and the community, and the cost of residential care, which many of these children require, is $80,000 to $100,000 per year.[8]

While admitting that autism rates seemed to be increasing at alarming levels, the CDC official attributed the spiraling growth to the broadened definitions of autism, increased awareness of the condition and other factors.[4]

WHY THE INCREASE?

When the Government Reform Committee of the U.S. House of Representatives convened a hearing on "Autism: Present Challenges, Future Needs—Why the Increased Rates?", the committee chairman shared his own opinion about the alarming rise in autism cases at the beginning of the hearing.

U.S. Representative Dan Burton, whose grandson developed autism within ten days of receiving seven immunizations in five shots, was the first to speak at the hearing. He said:

> When asked about the increased rates in autism, many will immediately discount that there even is an increase. Even though the latest statistics from the Department of Education show increased rates in every state. Others will say the increase is due to better diagnostic skills. Others will say it is because the diagnostic category was expanded.
>
> California has reported a 273 percent increase in children with autism since 1988. As for this increase,

21 percent of all autistic children in California live in the 29th district.

Florida has reported a 571 percent increase in autism. Maryland has reported a 513 percent increase between 1993 and 1998. You can't attribute all of that to better diagnostic skills.

In 1999, there were 2,462 children ages 3 to 21 in Indiana diagnosed with autism. That is one-fourth of one percent of all the school children in Indiana, or one in four hundred. Twenty-three percent of these children live in the 6th district. *This increase is not just better counting.*

If we want to find a cure, we must first look to the cause. We must do this now before our health and education systems are bankrupted, and before more of our nation's children are locked inside themselves with this disease.[9]

I believe that if alarming numbers such as those for the ADD, ADHD and autism epidemics had hit the media for chicken pox or measles, the nation would have risen up in arms and demanded that something be done.

This is even more alarming when you understand that the outcome for children with autism is often very dismal. Once erroneously called juvenile schizophrenia, the condition was considered absolutely incurable and untreatable. Victims of autism were routinely institutionalized and virtually forgotten in the nation's mental asylums.

Merriam-Webster's dictionary defines *autism* as "a mental disorder originating in infancy that is characterized by self-absorption, inability to interact socially, repetitive behavior and language dysfunction (as echolalia [strictly repetitive or imitative speech, often without regard to the meaning of the words or sounds])."[10]

The definition of autism was updated in recent years to

include a number of similar disorders collectively called autism syndrome or "Autistic Spectrum Disorders." According to the Autism-PDD (Pervasive Developmental Disorder) Network, "The diagnosis of autism is made when specified number of characteristics listed in the *DSM-IV* are present, in ranges inappropriate for the child's age. Autism diagnosis usually occurs between the ages three and five."[11]

WHAT CAUSES AUTISM?

No one knows for certain what causes autism in infants and young children. A growing body of scientific evidence and cataloged reports of personal experiences lend support to key theories about the condition's primary and secondary sources.

Initially, the medical community rejected its early belief that autism was caused by "refrigerator mothers" who failed to show affection for their children or who were abusive. Later it decided that autism was a psychiatric or mental problem related to mental retardation.

Current research points toward some common risk areas that may potentially cause autism, ADD and ADHD. Researchers appear to be divided into two camps.

The majority considers that autism is related to metabolic or allergic reactions caused by diet, gastrointestinal problems, hormonal imbalances and yeast infestations. The late Dr. Ben F. Feingold and Dr. William G. Crook have provided some invaluable insights into the interaction of allergies and dietary and nutritional factors with metabolic problems associated with ADD, ADHD and autistic spectrum disorders.[12] We'll take a closer look at their findings and recommendations later in this book.

Other medical specialists, such as Dr. Michael Goldberg, believe autism can be traced to the improper function or regulation of the body's immune system. The condition is complicated by metabolic problems on a secondary level.

In my mind, the most promising cutting-edge research draws from both camps. New findings point to the disruption of "G-alpha protein," which is a protein crucial to proper brain function and development.

A study by Dr. Mary N. Megson, a board-certified pediatrician and assistant professor of pediatrics at the Medical College of Virginia, suggested that autism may be linked to the pertussis toxin found in the DPT vaccine. She noted in her article:

> A study of sixty autistic children suggests that autism may be caused by inserting a G-alpha protein defect, the pertussis toxin found in the DPT vaccine, into genetically at-risk children.
>
> ...The far-reaching metabolic consequences [of the blocked neurotransmission it causes] may be enormous, with potential links to not only autism, but dyslexia, attention-deficit hyperactivity disorder (ADHD), bipolar disorder, schizophrenia, chronic fatigue syndrome, fibromyalgia, Type II hyperlipidemia, gluten enteropathy, cancer of the mucous-secreting glands and autoimmune disorders including muscular dystrophy and rheumatoid arthritis. [13]

Dr. Megson suspects that unrecognized allergic reactions to childhood immunizations combined with the introduction of certain foreign cells (called antigens) and toxins are culprits in many childhood distresses. (See chapter 8.) The G-alpha protein defect depletes the child's body of naturally occurring vitamin A, and it disrupts the immune system. Dr. Megson noted a research study conducted by Scrimshaw and others in 1968 that reported the lack of vitamin A is directly linked to infections. The authors of the study said, "No nutritional deficiency in the animal kingdom is more consistently synergistic with infection than that of vitamin A."[14]

SUPPLEMENTATION STRATEGIES

This view is strongly supported by very recent medical research and international health data collected by UNICEF, a relief organization of the United Nations:

> Three separate trials of children hospitalized with measles—one as early as 1932—showed that children died much less often when given high-dose vitamin A than those not given supplements. The consistent results suggest that boosting vitamin A can rapidly help cells repair and resist infection, thereby saving lives.[15]

Perhaps most interesting of all, Dr. Megson's research indicates that a natural form of vitamin A occurring in cod liver oil appears to "reconnect" the retinoid receptors in cells, which is critical for vision, sensory perception, language processing and attention. These happen to be key areas damaged in autistic children.

A link between intestinal disorders and autism has been suspected for some time. Previous improvements with some autistic children who received intravenous and sublingual doses of secretin seemed to indicate metabolic problems in the gut. Secretin is a hormone normally present in mammals but conspicuously absent in many autistic children.

TWO STORIES OF HOPE

Research by Dr. Megson and others reveal this is but part of the problem. Her findings offer hope for children who exhibit autistic symptoms, especially those who are treated early. She described two interesting case histories in her article:

> My earliest evidence came from a ten-year-old boy diagnosed with autism by *DSM-IV* criteria. The patient's parents suspect he has been reading since age four, but his inability to communicate made this

unverifiable. Over an eight-year period of regular visits I had never heard him speak. Standardized IQ tests revealed moderate mental retardation…

…I started the boy on cod liver oil (5,000 IU of vitamin A, given in 2500 IU/bid) and a gluten-free diet. After one week, he began to sit farther from the television and to notice paintings on the walls at home. He had always gone out of his way to follow the sidewalk and driveway to meet the school bus.

On vitamin A, he began to run across the grass directly from the front door to the bus. After three weeks, he was given a single dose of Urocholine, an alpha muscarinic receptor agonist, to increase bile and pancreatic secretions and indirectly stimulate hippocampal retinoid receptors. It has minimal cardiac effect, is FDA approved, has been used safely in children since the 1970s for reflux, and does not cross the blood-brain barrier, unlike secretin…

Thirty minutes after administration of the Urocholine, the patient, who was sitting in a chair, swung his feet over the side, pointed to a glass candy jar on my shelf and said, "May I have the red Jolly Rancher please?" He had read the label on the candy in the clear jar. These were the first words he had spoken in eight years and the first proof he could read. We took him outside and he said, "The leaves, the leaves on the tree are green! I see! I see!"…

In this child's case, after several weeks of treatment with vitamin A in cod liver oil, 3500 IU/day, the Urocholine acted like a switch. When absorbed, he immediately became socially engaged, made excellent eye contact, hugged his mother tightly and said, "I love you so much," looking her in the face. At that point we both realized that this boy had a blocked pathway. The change in language and social interaction was dramatic and immediate. Yet he reverted to the pre-treatment state of silence when the dose wore off. On lower daily doses of Urocholine (12.5 mg. bid) along with the vitamin A, his language and social interactions have continued to progress, albeit slowly. [16]

The second case involved a child demonstrating the first signs of an autistic spectrum disorder:

[A mother in Kentucky] was frantic because her four-teen-month-old infant had stopped making eye contact, began to stare at lights and fans, stopped cooing and laughing and no longer turned to sound after early normal development. The mother reported she was night blind and had irritable bowel syndrome. By mother's report, the infant was weaned and placed on standard formula, which was tolerated well. An audiological evaluation revealed normal auditory brainstem responses and tympanograms. The child went to pediatric ophthalmologist, who stated the child was farsighted. The exam was otherwise normal. The doctor was unable to get the infant to track in daylight, but when he placed an amber screen in front of his eyes he would easily track all objects.

I spoke with the child's pediatrician who obtained a vitamin A level. The value was 26ug/dl (normal is 30–90ug/dl). I instructed the mother to add 0.85 cc of CLO (Vitamins A/D) of cod liver oil to a bottle that night, and 0.85 cc CLO to a bottle at 11 A.M. the next day. When the baby woke from his nap, he was back to normal, smiling, laughing, turning to sound, and tracking objects. As a developmental pediatrician, I have followed his development. By his mother's reports, his receptive and expressive language, cognition, fine and gross motor skills are all normal for his age of nine months. He has remained on 0.85 cc CLO without significant increase in his vitamin A and D levels. He has had further immunizations without regression.[17]

At this writing, Dr. Megson was conducting a clinical trial using vitamin A in cod liver oil vs. placebo in a double-blind, crossover study. Once the data is collected from the trial, a second trial will begin using the combination of vitamin A and Urocholine.

Until these and other studies are complete, Dr. Megson's findings and hypotheses officially should be considered hypothetical and anecdotal, and in no way should be used in place of the informed judgment of your medical providers when making decisions concerning healthcare.

FACING A TIDE OF NEGATIVITY

There is hope, but I'm concerned that parents of autistic children may face a tide of negative viewpoints, comments and predictions that continue to dominate the health arena. The Autism-PDD (Pervasive Development Disorder) Network, a major parent support group, warns parents:

> The autism prognosis is startlingly grim and consistent across a broad range of studies—about 2 percent will attain normal functioning, with perhaps 40 percent labeled high-functioning autistic. These high-functioning autistic [children] generally show some oddities of behavior, and have few or no personal friends. Yet, with appropriate intervention, many of the autism behaviors can be positively changed, even to the point that the child or adult may appear, to the untrained person, to no longer have autism. Like any other family faced with this diagnosis, as you explore the options and resources available in your community, you will find on the one hand the unlimited potential your child has, and, on the other, the many

limits others try to place on their future. This is where a parent, facing a system with many flaws and pitfalls, must not compromise their vision of their child's future.[18]

Things have changed dramatically since the "dark years" when the public rarely heard anything about autism. When it did, autism was characterized as a hopeless mental condition from which there was no return to any measure of normalcy.

MOVIES RAISED PUBLIC AWARENESS OF AUTISM

Major theatrical releases such as *Mercury Rising* with Bruce Willis and *Rain Man* with Tom Cruise and Dustin Hoffman have raised public awareness of the problem. In addition, a number of prominent sports figures and entertainment personalities have launched public campaigns and established nonprofit foundations to fund research and services after their own families were affected by autism. Such high-profile endeavors have brought help and comfort to distraught parents who hear the dreaded diagnosis of autism spoken over their children.

Dr. Robert S. Mendelsohn made an observation that applies directly to anyone seeking hope and help for an autistic or a child with autistic-like symptoms:

> ...when doctors are compared with other people in evaluating retarded or other handicapped persons, those who always give the most dismal predictions and the lowest evaluations are doctors. Nurses are the next lowest, followed by psychologists. The group that always gives the most optimistic evaluation is the parents. When I'm faced with a doctor who tells me a child can't do certain things and parents who tell me that the child can do them, I always listen to the par-

ents. I really don't care which group is right or wrong. It's the attitude that counts. Whatever attitude is reinforced and encouraged will prove true.[19]

In the meantime, there are things you can do to avoid the G-protein problem. Begin by making sure your children have adequate amounts of vitamin A from cod liver oil. Vitamin A palmitate, the form found in most vitamin supplements, is not easily absorbed by youngsters with the pre-existing digestive problems so common among those whom Dr. Megson believes are most at risk.

If you plan to have your children immunized, wait as long as possible to allow plenty of time for their nervous systems to mature. Space out the injections if possible, and have multiple shots given individually (e.g., MMR and DPT).

ATTACK THE PROBLEM ON SEVERAL FRONTS

If your child is already battling autism or autistic-like symptoms, don't let despair paralyze you. Aggressively attack the problem on several fronts:

❑ Adjust your child's diet to eliminate every potential problem food or substance.

❑ Make sure your child receives proper amounts of vitamin A from cod liver oil (1 to 2 tablespoons daily) and the natural form of the B-complex vitamins, vitamin C and zinc.

❑ Early behavioral intervention is crucial for maximum potential. Immediately begin specialized training designed specifically for autistic children. Once your child is diagnosed with autism, he becomes eligible for a wide range of services and educational support. Investigate and get involved in one of the nationally recognized intervention programs specifically designed for autistic children, such as TREATT, the Lovass Method and the "Floor Time" behavioral therapy developed by Dr. Stanley L. Greenspan. Remember that these programs are not mutually exclusive—discover and use the parts of each program that produce results for your child.

❑ If you suspect your child is allergic to foods, dyes or other elements in your home or environment, have him tested by a reputable healthcare provider, preferably one who specializes in those areas.

❑ Link up with those who have made the journey before you. Parent support groups and national organizations such as the Autism Society of America, Families for Early Autism Treatment (FEAT) and the Autism-PDD Network can provide valuable information and save you a great deal of needless delay, pain and frustration. Most importantly, they will help you find and receive all the assistance available to you through the local school system and various health agencies in your area. A growing number of private foundations are joining the more traditional government sources funding research and providing services to families with one or more autistic members.

❑ Resist the temptation to measure your child against others. Focus on helping your child continue on the "learning curve" so he can fulfill his individual potential. No one really knows how far your child can go, so don't allow anyone to put limits on your child.

❑ Find qualified home health aides or workers who can bring their specialized services into your home. This will strengthen and reinforce the things your child learns at school, and it will provide a much-needed mental, spiritual and physical break for you as a parent.

All that is needed for many autistic children is the stimulus or boost to "reconnect" their minds with the ability to express their thoughts. When this happens we often see surprising results. For example, Britain's National Spastic Society invited a nonverbal autistic boy from India to London after he wrote five books in just two years.

"BOWLING" WITH AUTISTIC LITERARY GENIUS

Raj Rishi Mukhopadhyay, from the southern city of Bangalore, "bowled over" the Society with his literary genius. The BBC (British Broadcasting Channel) produced a fifty-minute documentary on Raj, and the *Telegraph*, an Indian newspaper, reported that experts in Britain wanted to study and assess his literary prowess.

Raj's own writings include books on poetry and a lyrical eighty-page autobiography in English, which talks about how he broke through the barrier of autism and began to negotiate with the world outside.

"He is constantly giving an insight into the feelings of an autist which we never had before," said a doctor in Bangalore, where, with the help of the Spastic Society of India, the Speech and Hearing Society and, of course, his mother, he has been nurturing his skills.

Raj's mother first noticed signs of his ability to communicate when he was just four.

"Like most parents, I was frightened of his condition. But I was not ready to give up. I would speak to him constantly and tell stories, whether or not he paid attention. He had a fixation for calendars. Then, one day, I asked him to point out the numbers and he did. I suddenly realized we could communicate with each other," said Soma Mukhopadhyay, Raj's mother.

She then started teaching Raj the English alphabet, and soon enough, Raj became a voracious reader.

Today Raj writes prose that can leave the reader spell-bound. "Not in abstract existence of the impossible world of dreams but a hope for a concrete dream of this book reaching those who would like to understand us through me..." says the epilogue of Raj's autobiography.[20]

Thank God for the gift in your child, and trust Him for the strength to be your child's most vocal and diligent earthly advocate.

EIGHT

America's
Love Affair With
Mass Immunizations

Most children in the United States *receive thirty-three doses of ten different vaccines before they reach age five*, according to a report aired by CBS News in September 2000. The vaccines reportedly provide protection for "everything from childhood diseases like chicken pox to adult diseases like hepatitis B."[1]

Meanwhile, for decades a growing number of reputable researchers and medical doctors have been suggesting that, in addition to immunities, these vaccines may provide some things that are much less desirable. For some children, they may be causing mental retardation, SIDS, paralysis and death.

New research appears to implicate childhood immunizations as the suspected cause of a host of autoimmune diseases in genetically susceptible individuals. The list includes cancer, leukemia, rheumatoid arthritis, multiple sclerosis, Lou Gehrig's disease, lupus erythematosus, Guillain-Barré syndrome, autistic spectrum disorders and even ADHD.[2]

One element of mass immunization distresses me. We live in the United States of America, a nation governed by constitutional principles protecting the rights of individuals from governmental oppression. Yet, parents who dare to question the wisdom of immunizing their children can face strong-arm tactics from school districts that include forced removal of their children and even criminal prosecution! The only course left to many of them is legal action in courts—courts that could appear to demonstrate a strong bias toward the medical establishment and the "party line."

Something is seriously wrong with a system that makes conscientious and thoughtful parents feel like criminals because they want to protect their children from what they believe is a very risky and unnecessary medical procedure.

MIXED SIGNALS?

The natural tendency for concerned parents is to consult with a trusted family physician for advice and assistance in wading through the conflicting evidence. Unfortunately, even the medical community seems to be giving mixed signals. (This may be due to the obvious conflict of interest between the medical professionals and the high profits generated by mass immunizations and the considerable influence wielded by pharmaceutical giants.)

A resolution was presented at the 1982 Forum of the American Academy of Pediatrics (AAP) proposing that pediatricians should help inform parents about the risks as well as the supposed benefits of immunizations. This is what the proposal said in part:

> [The] AAP [shall] make available in clear, concise language information which a reasonable parent would want to know about the benefits and risks of routine immunizations, the risks of vaccine preventable diseases and the management of common adverse reactions to immunizations.

The late Dr. Mendelsohn responded to the outcome by saying, "Apparently the doctors assembled did not believe that 'reasonable parents' were entitled to this kind of information because they *rejected the resolution!*"[3]

Thousands of parents in the United States, Great Britain, Germany and many other nations refuse to accept the official "party line" of the medical and pharmaceutical communities about the total safety of compulsory immunizations. Why? They believe their children were *irreparably harmed or killed* by complications from childhood immunizations.

More and more of them are banding together to establish advocacy organizations and legislative lobby groups. They are also financing lawsuits against officials in school districts, state health departments and federal agencies when necessary.

THEY WANT TO KNOW WHY

These parents want to know why childhood cases of autism have increased 500 percent in just two decades. They also want to know why juvenile cases of asthma jumped 100 percent and juvenile diabetes levels rocketed to the 200 percent mark. For the most part, the persistent questions of these parents are answered by little more than a mountain of excuses and official scorn by the medical establishment. It doesn't matter. These parents and others like them are on a crusade for life.

In the meantime, the World Health Organization is quietly stating what a growing minority of medical experts in the U.S. believe is the scientifically based truth about disease and immunizations.

Research has clearly shown that *adequate amounts of vitamin A, zinc and other essential nutrients* significantly reduce the risk and mortality rates of diseases such as measles and of outbreaks of diarrhea. This is especially true in so-called Third World nations and other areas where malnutrition and poor sanitation conditions exist.[4] Recent research indicates that vitamin A in particular may even lower the risk that HIV/AIDS mothers will pass on the disease to their babies at childbirth.[5]

While the World Health Organization still endorses immunizations in those countries, it is citing scientific research that shows proper nutrition is the first line of defense against many viral and bacterial diseases in so-called Third World nations.

OBSCENE SEIZURE AND THE CUSTODY OF STRANGERS

Who should have the authority to weigh the potential benefits against the potential risks of immunizations for *your child?* Unfortunately, the decision has already been made for most of us.

In many, if not most, states, a government medical official has already *made all the decisions for you* concerning when, what, how and how many immunizations your children will receive. If you disagree, your children will be denied access to public education, including colleges and universities.

Don't be surprised if you wake up to the knock of a sheriff's deputy with a bench warrant to remove your school-age children from your home just to make sure they receive those vaccinations! Does this sound far-fetched? It has happened.

I read in one article that school officials in Utica, New York, had threatened the parents of seventy-seven middle school students with forcible removal of their children unless they agreed to submit them to vaccination with the highly controversial hepatitis B vaccine. If the parents refused, officials were prepared to forcibly remove the children from their homes and turn them over to Child

Protective Services on the legal grounds of parental neglect within two weeks![6] Remember: This didn't happen in some repressive totalitarian state on another continent. It took place on American soil.

In response, Jane M. Orient, M.D., executive director of American Physicians and Surgeons, spoke out in the same article on behalf of the families and said, "It's obscene to seize a child and force him to the custody of strangers just because his parents refuse medical treatment they think is unnecessary or even dangerous. Parents, not…government bureaucrats, should make decisions about their children's medical care."[7]

Officials often say they are acting in the child's best interest, but the claim is questionable at best in cases where the scientific evidence suggests otherwise. Dr. Orient warned that the latest vaccination rage, the hepatitis B vaccine, "…is a potential death sentence for some children. Government studies show that children under the age of fourteen are three times more likely to die or suffer adverse reactions after receiving hepatitis B vaccine than to catch the disease itself."[8]

In spite of the evidence, zealous immunization advocates determined to eradicate disease, even if the effort kills and maims more victims than the disease, have pressed to make the hepatitis B vaccine the latest addition to the compulsory immunization laws of most states.

Ironically, hepatitis B is almost exclusively an adult disease primarily spread through body fluids among those with multiple sex partners, those who use intravenous drugs or those whose occupations expose them to blood. Children face a very low risk of exposure unless they are infected by their mother at birth.

Most of the children in the United States are required to receive several common immunizations, including (but not limited to):

- ❏ *DTaP/DPT/DTPH* (One of three combined-vaccines: diphtheria-tetanus-acellular pertussis, which is a less reactive modification of DPT/diphtheria-pertussis-tetanus/diphtheria-tetanus-pertussis-hemophilus influenza type B).

- ❏ *MMR* (measles-mumps-rubella)

- ❏ *OPV* (oral polio vaccine—live-virus type)

- ❏ *"Conjugated" HIB* (hemophilus influenza type B)

- ❏ *Hepatitis B*

- ❏ *Chicken pox* (Many states have added or are considering vaccinations for chicken pox and many other lesser diseases as well.)

Perhaps the first question to consider is obvious: Have compulsory immunizations *really* controlled or eliminated childhood diseases? If you believe the continual claims of government and medical spokesmen and state health departments, the nation's childhood immunization programs are man's savior from disease.

According to "cause of death" statistics from Metropolitan Life Insurance Company recorded from 1911 to 1935, four diseases topped the list as causes of death for children aged one to fourteen: diphtheria, measles, scarlet fever and whooping cough.[9]

CHILDHOOD DISEASES DROPPED 95 PERCENT BEFORE IMMUNIZATIONS!

The death rate from these four leading childhood diseases declined from forty-five per one hundred thousand in 1911 to twenty-eight per one hundred thousand in 1935—or a *decrease of 81 percent!* By 1945, the combined death rate from these diseases had dropped further to seven per one hundred thousand.[10] This amounts to a *total decline* in deaths from the top four childhood diseases of *95 percent*—years *before* the mass immunization programs began in the United States.[11]

Perhaps the best way to make sense of the most common immunizations is to examine diseases they allegedly eliminate or control as well.

MEASLES (RUBEOLA OR "ENGLISH MEASLES")

Measles (rubeola or "English measles") is a common childhood illness *treated with bed rest and plenty of fluids.* Most people who attended school in the 1950s and early 1960s remember staying home from class to recover from the measles. They usually aren't remarkable memories, because the symptoms of the disease aren't really remarkable as long as a child was well-nourished and living in sanitary conditions.

Once a child contracts measles, he gains *lifetime immunity.* The only dangerous derivative of the measles virus is *measles encephalitis*, which is said to happen only once in one thousand cases of measles.

Dr. Mendelsohn believed that this statistic could *only be applied to children living in conditions of poverty or malnutrition.* Odds of one in ten thousand or one in one hundred thousand are more likely in the U.S. and other developed countries![12] Ironically, Dr. Mendelsohn and other medical authorities and researchers claim the immunization itself carries a high risk of causing measles encephalitis, encephalopathy (or brain dysfunction) and the nearly always fatal SSPE, or subacute sclerosing panencephalitis (which hardens brain matter).[13]

The measles serum has a very checkered history for these reasons:

IT DOESN'T SEEM TO WORK.

According to a U.S. Centers for Disease Control report, 40 percent of all cases of measles reported in 1989 were in *vaccinated individuals* or could be attributed to "primary measles vaccine failure."[14] These same figures showed up in the fourteen measles outbreaks in 1977.[15]

One World Health Organization (WHO) study said people who have been vaccinated against measles are fourteen times more likely to contract measles than those who have not![16] One official with the Centers for Disease Control said that in some measles outbreaks, "...over 95 percent have a history of vaccination."[17]

IF THE VACCINATION DOES OFFER PROTECTION TO A PORTION OF THE POPULATION, THOSE WHO DO GET VACCINATED EVIDENTLY HAVE ONLY LIMITED BENEFIT.

Blood tests show no evidence of measles antibodies after approximately four years. After measles outbreaks occurred among fully immunized high school and college students, the Immunization Practices Advisory Committee recommended in 1989 that *two doses* of measles vaccine be required.

> Since 1990, colleges and universities in twenty-two states established a "Pre-matriculation Immunization Requirement" forcing students to get two measles shots before they can matriculate from college! (This in spite of scientific evidence that two doses of the vaccine are no more effective than one.)[18]

RECENT RESEARCH REPEATEDLY POINTS TO THE MEASLES COMPONENT OF THE MMR VACCINE AS A POSSIBLE SOURCE OF THE EXPLODING AUTISM EPIDEMIC SWEEPING THROUGH THE NATION.

Vijendra K. Singh, Ph.D., of the Department of Biology and Biotechnology Center at Utah State University, testified before a congressional committee that in a study of four hundred people (composed of those diagnosed with autism and a control group exhibiting no symptoms of autistic spectrum disorders), she found a brain protein known as myelin basic protein (MBP) in 65 to 85 percent of autistic children, but only rarely (0 to 5 percent) in normal children.

Further investigation verified that the autoantibodies were created as part of a hyper-immune response to a virus—*specifically for the measles virus (MV).* Dr. Singh summarized her testimony with these astounding statements: *"This was most probably the first laboratory-based evidence to link measles virus and/or MMR vaccine to auto-immunity in children with autism. Collectively, these observations led me to speculate that autism may be caused by a measles- or MMR vaccine-induced autoimmune response."*[19]

MUMPS

Mumps is a very contagious disease caused by a virus that focuses on the salivary glands on either side of the neck under the jaw. It causes painful swelling along the jaw line just below the ears, along with fever, headache, muscle aches and back pain. It may also cause swelling in testicles, ovaries and breasts.

The disease is uncomfortable but rarely serious. The painful swelling may diminish after the third day, and all symptoms disappear in about ten days. The downside, which is made even more dangerous by the delaying effect of the temporary immunity provided by childhood mumps immunization, is that about one-third of males *past the age of puberty* who contract mumps develop orchitis, or inflammation of one of the testes (it rarely affects both testicles).

The side effects of the mumps vaccine can be severe, including a risk of contracting viral meningitis, febrile seizures, unilateral nerve deafness and encephalitis.

RUBELLA (GERMAN MEASLES)

Rubella is a mild disease in children that does not require medical treatment. A child runs a fever and exhibits the symptoms of a cold and a sore throat at first. Then he or she develops a rash on the face and scalp that spreads to the arms and trunk of the body. Unlike measles, the spots in rubella, or "German measles," do not run together. With plenty of rest and fluids, the rash and the disease fade away after three days, leaving the child with permanent immunity.

The only real danger of rubella is that it may damage the unborn child of a mother who contracts the disease in the first trimester of pregnancy. In Dr. Mendelsohn's words, "This fear is used to justify the immunization of all children, boys and girls, as part of the MMR innoculation."[20]

Many health providers feel that childhood immunizations deprive young women of the lifelong immunity they would have received from the rubella virus in harmless childhood stage of life, for the immunizations do not always last. This is one of the really irritating problems plaguing the immunization program—most of the people who come down with this and other childhood diseases consistently show proof of previous vaccinations. As demonstrated elsewhere, this is the problem behind the re-vaccination of college students.

Recent studies have linked the new rubella vaccine introduced in 1979 with chronic fatigue syndrome (also known as the Epstein-Barr virus). This link was first reported in the United States in 1982.[21] Although many hospitals require employees (including obstetricians and pediatricians) to take the rubella vaccine, a study appearing in the *Journal of the American Medical Association* noted that nine of every ten obstetricians and more than two-thirds of pediatricians refused to take the vaccine.[22] One can only wonder why they would take such an action. We may never know, but it seems to beg the need for some explanation by these physicians who are most familiar with the possible risks involved.

DIPHTHERIA

Diphtheria is a *bacterial* disease that was widely feared in the previous century when antibiotics were unavailable. The disease was already disappearing *before* a vaccine became available (probably due to better nutrition, cleaner water sources and more sanitary living conditions nationwide and particularly in larger cities).

Only five people contracted diphtheria in 1980; only *four* cases appeared in 1992. The disappearance of this disease *before* the introduction of vaccines has been explained and documented earlier using insurance tables. Obviously the disease rarely occurs. When it does, it is effectively treated with modern antibiotics. Nevertheless, we continue to immunize children against it today.

The diphtheria component of the DPT and DTaP vaccine has not been shown to cause serious short-term side effects. Its long-term effects—as with any injection of foreign bodies into the human body—remain totally unknown. Formaldehyde is used to "stabilize" the diphtheria vaccine, but the dangers of formaldehyde as a carcinogen are well documented. The use of this chemical (and many others such as mercury and aluminum) in vaccine production will be discussed at greater length later in this book with the full documentation it deserves.

In 1975, the Bureau of Biologics and the FDA concluded in an official report that diphtheria toxoid (which is the "safe" form of the disease used for vaccination) "...is not as effective an immunizing agent as might be anticipated." The report also acknowledged that those who received the vaccination could still contract the disease, noting "the permanence of immunity induced by the toxoid...is open to question."[23] The report noted that about 50 percent of all the people who contract diphtheria appear to have been fully vaccinated!

WHOOPING COUGH (PERTUSSIS)

Whooping cough (pertussis) is spread by airborne bacteria from an infected person and is extremely contagious. Common cold symptoms surface approximately seven to ten days after exposure, followed by a severe cough at night. Later the cough occurs in the daytime, characterized by sudden outbursts of convulsive coughing called "paroxysmal coughing." This coughing can frighten parents when their child coughs a dozen times with each breath, especially if his face darkens to a bluish or purple hue. The disease gets its name from the whooping noise that a victim makes when he or she takes in breath at the end of each coughing bout.

The disease can strike any age group. Currently between one thousand to three thousand cases of whooping cough occur per year, with between five and twenty deaths annually across the nation. *Although the disease is very distressing to young victims and their parents, the incidence of death is virtually negligible.* Consistent findings show this vaccine does tend to lower incidences of outbreak cases. Yet it is notorious for "wearing out" after a few years and for being totally ineffective very often.

Consult a doctor if an *infant* comes down with whooping cough. Hospital care may be required to protect the child from the threat of exhaustion from coughing and pneumonia.

The pertussis or whooping cough component of the DPT vaccine is one of the most controversial of all vaccines. Many consider it to be unpredictable, toxic and questionable in its ability to actually prevent infection with the disease.

Multiple research studies link the pertussis vaccine (whether given alone or as part of a DPT combination) with acute brain injury, anaphylactic shock, shock-collapse, inconsolable crying, febrile seizures, convulsions, sudden infant death syndrome (SIDS), severe and moderate encephalopathy, severe mental retardation, cerebral palsy, blindness, irreversible brain damage, myoclonic twitching, paralysis, infantile spasms, epilepsy and *hyperactivity*.[24]

Most parents of vaccinated children probably won't be surprised by these findings. Researchers found that 93 percent of the infants who received the DPT shot experienced moderate to severe reactions within forty-eight hours of inoculation![25] That alone is alarming.

I urge special caution if you or your child has a history of allergies or seizures. The pertussis toxin has another name— HSF, or "histamine sensitizing factor." That means it dramatically increases the human body's sensitivity to the effects of histamine. If your child has severe allergies (especially toward milk or dairy products), he or she may well have a hypersensitive immune system that could predispose him or her to a negative (and possibly violent) reaction to the pertussis vaccine.

One physician discovered a history of allergies with twenty of thirty-five children who reacted to the DPT-polio vaccine with persistent screaming, shock/collapse or convulsions. Another noted that "infants with a family history of fits or allergic conditions are more likely to become ill after vaccination than those without such a history."[26]

Although 95 percent of the children in the United States have been vaccinated against whooping cough, the nation still records about three thousand cases per year, and the vaccine's effect seems to wear off in a few years.[27]

Despite continuous official disclaimers, numerous research studies also point to a probable connection between the pertussis vaccine used in the U.S. until recently and the rise in autistic spectrum disorders.

Authors Harris L. Coulter, Ph.D., and Barbara Loe Fisher, cofounder and president of the National Vaccine Information

Center, wrote in their book *A Shot in the Dark*, "The phenomenon of early-infantile autism was first observed and discussed by physicians in the early 1940s, a few years after the pertussis vaccine became more widely used in the United States." Noting "…the brain appears to be isolated from the senses in autistic children," the authors wrote:

> The parallel to certain cases of pertussis vaccine damage is striking…Both *autism* and *minimal brain damage* [*ADD* or *ADHD*], as discussed previously, suggest a breakdown in the brain's ability to receive and process information through the senses. The relationship of autism to pertussis-vaccine damage deserves further investigation.
>
> Some autistic children share another trait with the minimally brain damaged—*a tendency to be hyperactive* with all of the associated emotional and behavioral problems.[28]

As noted in the previous chapter, very recent research by Dr. Mary Megson pointedly implicates the pertussis vaccine as a possible toxic cause of autism that "inserts a G-alpha protein defect" into genetically at-risk children. This appears to be particularly linked to individuals with a family history of night blindness or irritable bowel syndrome.[29]

Jamie Murphy, author of *What Every Parent Should Know About Childhood Immunization*, noted, "Because whooping cough has become milder in some countries of Europe since about 1970, and because of the ineffectiveness of the triple vaccine, DPT vaccinations were halted in West Germany in 1976 and in Sweden in 1979."[30]

Although reported cases of whooping cough rose after the immunizations were discontinued, the *death rate* from the disease remained at the same low levels present when the immunizations were in full swing. Perhaps more importantly, the rates of death or health complications *from the DPT shot* dropped to zero. Pertussis appears to be a cyclical disease with cases rising in numbers every three or four years—whether its victims are vaccinated or not.[31]

Japanese researchers responded to the DPT crisis by developing a much safer "purified pertussis vaccine" in the late 1970s, but U.S. public health officials *waited fifteen years* before licensing the acellular pertussis vaccine for American babies. Unfortunately, the DTaP vaccine is more expensive than the DPT vaccine, and the FDA and vaccine manufacturers refused to take the crude and more dangerous whole cell pertussis vaccine off the market.[32]

This action was even less defensible when clinical trials held in the previous decade demonstrated that the DTaP vaccine were 82 to 96 percent effective, while the crude and toxic DPT vaccine demonstrated a wildly erratic efficiency rate bouncing between 36 to 96 percent. Serious reactions continued to result with the DTaP vaccine, but they occurred significantly less often.[33]

TETANUS

Tetanus is a nervous-system disorder spawned by spores trapped in wounds that have not been properly cleaned. It causes body muscles to tighten and jaw muscles to go into spasms; it also triggers convulsions, headaches and depression. Untreated, the condition produces death 50 percent of the time. With proper treatment, victims completely recover in 80 percent of all cases.

Evidently, the disease is virtually 100 percent avoidable when wounds are properly cleaned. Tetanus declined among military personnel from 205 cases per 100,000 wounds in the Civil War to .44 cases per 100,000 wounds during World War II. The disease was rapidly declining long before a vaccine was developed. Throughout World War II, only twelve cases of tetanus were recorded! (Four of the cases involved individuals who were "adequately" vaccinated.) Perhaps this explains why some doctors report that the tetanus toxoid (the "safe" version of the toxin used as a vaccine) does not provide protection.[34]

The tetanus vaccine can have some painful complications, the most serious being demyelinating neuropathy (a degenerative condition of the nervous system), anaphylactic shock and seriously lowered T-lymphocyte rations, a crucial component of a healthy immune system. It appears this is yet another example of forcing a little-needed vaccine with potentially harmful side effects into the bodies of young children in the name of "100 percent immunization" without justification.

HEPATITIS B

The newest addition to the list of mandated childhood vaccinations may prove the most difficult to understand. The logic of wanting to protect children from polio or whooping cough is understandable.

In my opinion, there seems to be far less logic for forcing parents in America to submit their children to the injection of a toxic serum to "protect" them from a liver disease primarily limited to IV drug users and those with multiple sex partners. Also at risk are health workers who are regularly exposed to human blood products and hemophiliacs who are dependent upon frequent blood transfusions.

In 1991, the Centers for Disease Control and the American Association of Pediatricians launched an aggressive campaign to add the hepatitis B vaccine to the list of recommended and government-funded childhood vaccines. The effort was successful, and most of America's children must receive this toxic serum or be denied access to public education. I personally believe that this effort needlessly placed millions of infants at risk. I will discuss this matter in greater detail later on.

POLIOMYELITIS (POLIO)

Polio was the scourge of the 1940s, and it was the disease that condemned a U.S. president to a wheelchair. The development of the polio vaccine launched a national high-powered immunization campaign. Ironically, the vaccines developed to "protect" America's population from polio eventually may have become *its most likely cause!*

Dr. Jonas Salk, an American physician and micro-biologist, introduced a "killed-virus" vaccine against polio in 1955, but the death rate from the disease had already declined 47 percent in the United States from 1923 to 1953. The disease demonstrated a similar decline in England and other European nations as well.

Ironically, the number of reported polio cases was significantly higher *after* the mass inoculations than *before!* In fact, they may have more than *doubled* in the United States as a whole.[35] Evidently, the "live virus" vaccine introduced four years later by Albert Sabin was little better. The *Washington Post* reported in September 1976 that Dr. Jonas Salk had testified that the live-virus vaccine was "the principle if not sole cause" of all reported polio cases in the United States since 1961.[36] Even the Centers for Disease Control admitted that the live-virus polio vaccine was the primary cause of polio in the United States![37]

If the polio vaccine causes polio and the disease was disappearing on its own, then why did the government demand that we use it?

MONKEY VIRUS CONTAMINATION

It has been known for decades that the *simian virus 40 (SV40) grossly contaminated the oral polio vaccine administered to the U.S. school population prior to 1964!* One fear is this virus continues to contaminate polio vaccines used by pediatricians today because these vaccines are often made by passing serum products through African green monkey kidney cells. Recent evidence using advanced techniques uncovered molecular evidence of SV40 infections in tissue samples from four children born after 1982.[38] What is the significance of this discovery? Since the SV40 virus is a highly carcinogenic (cancer-causing) "latent or persistent monkey virus" known to cross-transmit to humans, it is feared that this virus can cause cancer in human hosts many years after it "hides" in human body cells. This virus is extremely difficult to discover.

According to Leon Chaitow, the English author of *Vaccination and Immunisation: Dangers, Delusions and Alternatives:*

> SV40-contaminated vaccines were used in millions of individuals, and this micro-organism, which is known to be capable of genetically altering other virus (especially let it be noted with Epstein-Barr and cytomegaloviruses) and cellular genetic material, entered the bodies of a generation now in young and middle adult life.[39]

Today, polio has all but disappeared. Should the paralytic form of the disease ever become active in someone's body, doctors do have drugs to deal with it. (Although they have some bad side effects, they appear to be nothing compared to the reported side effects of the polio vaccines!)

DEALING WITH THE FALLOUT

If you are disturbed by some of the information provided in this chapter, you are not alone. The general public is virtually unaware that mandatory vaccinations have harmed or killed so many children over the last four decades that Congress passed the National Childhood Vaccine Injury Acts of 1986, Public Law 99-660, to officially recognize the reality of vaccine-related injuries and deaths.

Its dual purpose was to establish safety provisions (which some claim has essentially degenerated into eager efforts to increase levels of immunization rather than make them safer) and to establish a no-fault federal compensation plan for individuals injured or killed by vaccines and their families.

Barbara Loe Fisher consulted and negotiated with the American Academy of Pediatrics, vaccine manufacturers and legislative staffs to create the no-fault compensation bill that became the National Childhood Vaccine Injury Act of 1986. She said:

> The fact that the [U.S. Claims] Court *turns down 75 percent of the claims* that are made is primarily due to the vigorous, well-financed opposition mounted by federal public health officials and Department of Justice lawyers. Since the National Childhood Vaccine Injury Act was passed in 1986, HHS officials and Justice Department lawyers have systematically gutted the law by passing federal regulations that narrow the criteria that special masters employed by the U.S. Claims Court may use to make awards to vaccine-injured children...
>
> As a result, by 1997 there was a $1 billion dollar surplus in the trust fund that is supposed to be used to provide financial support for individuals injured by mandated vaccines. Federal health officials continue to take actions to further limit the numbers of awards made for vaccine injuries because they do not want to admit that so many children and adults have been injured and killed by the vaccines they develop, license, regulate, and promote for mandatory use by all citizens.[40]

The fact is that most of the diseases listed above rarely kill under modern health and sanitation conditions. Although these diseases may cause significant discomfort for victims and their families, there is at least some evidence that those who contract such diseases seem likely to fully regain good health if they have access to adequate nutrition, sanitary living conditions and competent medical care if needed.

I'LL TAKE MY CHANCES!

It is my personal belief—let me emphasis this again—it is *my personal belief* that individuals can often fare better *with the disease* rather than through childhood immunizations. However, I do not presume to recommend that you adopt the same opinion solely on the basis of this book or any other single source of information.

Conduct your own thorough study of the available medical literature in books, on credible sites on the Internet and through consultations with competent health professionals before you make your own decisions.

As you know, my personal belief in the matter of immunizations is definitely a *minority* opinion among medical doctors and research scientists (in my mind, the existence of even *one* competent medical professional who shares my concern about vaccinations is enough to make responsible parents think twice about vaccinating their children). Therefore, it is vital that you come to your own conclusions based upon thorough study, consideration and consultation with your family physician.

One statement in the literature I've read continues to haunt me, and in large part it has led me to include the subject of immunizations in this book. In their chapter describing the evolution of mandatory immunizations in this country, authors Coulter and Fisher said:

> Curiously, the United States appears to be the only major Western nation with compulsory pertussis immunization...In fact, the only part of Europe where pertussis vaccination is universally imposed is the [former] Soviet Union and the formerly "iron curtain" countries of Poland, Hungary, and Czechoslovakia.

Mass vaccination in our "free society" is not voluntary. Since the repeal of the draft in the 1970s, *mandatory vaccination remains the only law that requires a citizen to risk his life for his country.*[41]

Perhaps the most alarming aspect of increasingly invasive mass immunizations is that the trend seems to be expanding at the same rate as runaway cancer. Coulter and Fisher warn:

More than *2,000 vaccines* are being created in government and drug company labs, vaccines such as live rotavirus (infant diarrhea), salmonella, strep, tuberculosis, gonorrhea, herpes, Epstein-Barr virus, hepatitis A, B, C, D, and E, and cholera. More than 50 different HIV vaccines are being developed to theoretically prevent AIDS, including a live HIV vaccine that will be inhaled and followed by an injection a week later. *Scientists are creating a genetically engineered super-vaccine to be squirted into the mouths of babies at the moment of birth that will inject raw DNA from 30 to 40 different viruses and bacteria directly into an infant's cells* and be time-released into the body throughout childhood. There is little question that federal and state health officials will try to pass regulations legally requiring that all citizens use many of these vaccines, including the AIDS vaccine.[42]

Perhaps it would be easier for critics to write off such commentary as reactionary and extreme if we didn't already have so many examples of such excessive executive force exercised by government employees against tax-paying parents who have little say in the formation of such regulations.

CDC PIN CUSHIONS

The "100 percent immunization at any cost" mind-set may well undermine the health, long-term welfare and constitutional freedoms of an entire nation if left unchecked. I'm convinced Gordon Steward, a leading European physician and respected professor of community medicine at the University of Glasgow, Scotland, was right when he said, "If the Centers for Disease Control has its way, *Americans and their children are going to become human pin cushions.*"[43]

The American public has no place to turn as long as the executive, judicial and legislative branches of government maintain such a close alliance with the medical and pharmaceutical communities that the value of objective "checks and balances" seems to be lost. The most prominent group left out of the "compulsory immunization profits party" may well be the vast majority of trusting American citizens and their children.

The goal of this chapter is not to persuade you to agree with my personal convictions. It is simply to provide you with some additional facts so you can make an *informed* decision. It seems that most doctors, educators and public health officials often provide information from only one side of the immunization issue.

Only informed parents have the moral, spiritual and ethical right to make life-and-death decisions concerning their children. For better or for worse, parents have the best shot at truly having their children's best interests in mind when they consider the pros and cons of childhood immunizations. Educate yourself before the last vestige of parental discretion is taken from you.

NINE

Heavy Metals
and Toxic Injections

It is time to add some additional information to our previous discussions of mandatory immunizations in this country. The information represents some of the latest research on the origins of autoimmune diseases and even of ADHD, ADD and autistic spectrum disorders. I must warn you that it is extensive and extremely controversial.

We are about to probe a nightmare of heavy metals and the possible contamination of many of the nation's immunization serums.

It includes the incredible revelation that for several decades, our state and federal governments have given our children immunizations using vaccines that may have contained highly toxic chemicals. Some are ranked among the government's "Top Twenty Hazardous Substances." Under certain circumstances, these substances can maim the body, incapacitate the human brain and nervous system and even kill.

Some who read this chapter will say I am absolutely wrong. Others will just as enthusiastically declare that I am right. Frankly, I felt compelled to include this information because I've seen too many children affected under circumstances too suspicious to sweep under the rug of political correctness. Regardless of its origin, we are experiencing an epidemic of biblical proportions, and *something has to change.* For my part, I felt honor-bound to provide you with the things I've ascertained as a biochemist and health researcher.

Before we go any further, I want to encourage you to examine every statement in this book and in other sources with a critical eye. Seek out more information on this subject from as many reputable sources as you can find, and draw your own informed opinions. Only then should you make decisions concerning vaccinations for yourself and your family. Ultimately, the decision is yours, so get the facts before you act.

To be honest, the majority opinion in the medical world is contrary to many of the things presented in this chapter—even though they are based on scientific research conducted by licensed physicians and distinguished medical research scientists. Doctors and scientists *do* disagree, and they do it often. There are obviously arguments to be made on both sides of this topic as well. This makes it even more crucial for us as parents to be *informed* decision makers.

The very idea that poisonous substances may be included in childhood vaccines can catch even medical professionals by surprise. Psychologist Bernard Rimland, founder of the Autism Research Institute in San Diego, California, and the parent of an adult autistic child, described his reaction when he first learned about the contents of some of the vaccines being injected into American children.

It happened in the late 1960s when one of Dr. Rimland's graduate students wrote a research paper noting that mercury poisoning mimicked many of the symptoms of autism. The student mentioned that acrodynia, or pink disease, caused a number of symptoms (including those of autism) that baffled the medical community until the cause was finally discovered: *mercury* contained in teething lotions and diaper powders! Dr. Rimland said:

> I remember thinking, Interesting...another mystery solved. But only of historical interest. How wrong I was!
>
> I had assumed, very naively as it turned out, that the FDA and the drug manufacturers would henceforth scrupulously avoid using mercury. I was aware that minute amounts of mercury, along with other toxins, such as aluminum and formaldehyde, were used as preservatives in vaccines, but, after all, I assumed, since everyone now knew that these substances are extremely toxic, those highly sophisticated vaccine-makers would not possibly use amounts which even approach dangerous levels. Bad guess![1]

FORTY-ONE TIMES THE "SAFE" ADULT LEVEL OF MERCURY!

Despite official studies claiming otherwise, many leaders feel convinced that there is a clear "cause and effect" relationship between certain childhood immunizations and the sudden onset of autism and other learning disabilities. Included among them is U.S. Representative Dan Burton from Indiana, who noted during congressional hearings that his grandson developed autistic symptoms after receiving a round of vaccinations. Representative Burton estimated that his grandson had received *forty-one times the amount of mercury considered safe for adults*—and all in *one day!*[2]

According to the "Position Paper of the Consensus Conference on the Mercury Detoxification of Autistic Children" released by the Autism Research Institute, "Some infants have been given, in one day, as much as one hundred times the maximum dosage of mercury permitted by the Environmental Protection Agency's standards, [which are] based on the weight of an adult." The paper noted that an infant's system is much less capable of dealing with toxins than an adult's.[3]

The source of mercury in vaccine serums is thimerosal, a preservative that consists of approximately 50 percent mercury. Although the FDA asked drug makers to begin removing thimerosal from vaccines in 1998, *fifty vaccines containing the preservative are still in use at this writing!*[4] (Note: The MMR vaccine is also controversial for its arguably dangerous measles virus, but this multiple vaccine *does not contain mercury* in the form of thimerosal.)

Dr. Rimland cited two studies confirming the risks associated with vaccines containing mercury:

> In one study, a single injection of hepatitis B vaccine significantly raised blood mercury levels in fifteen premature and fifteen full-term infants, and mercury levels were markedly higher in the preemies. Another study, by the Centers for Disease Control and Prevention, found a slight, but statistically significant, association between mercury from vaccines and neurological disorders.[5]

WEIGHED IN THE BALANCE?

Most parents do not want to do away with the immunization program, but they do want to make sure their children are not exposed to unsafe vaccines. The problem appears to be that almost any negative finding or theory that may lower the national vaccination rate is quickly attacked and silenced for fear it may harm the national immunization program.

In my mind, *the clear short-term and long-term danger to our children's health* far outweighs any government concern over the "success" of a federal immunization program!

It is a fact that *mercury* is ranked *number three* in the "Top 20 Hazardous Substances ATSDR/EPA Priority List" published annually by the Agency for Toxic Substances and

Disease Registry of the Centers For Disease Control![6]

When you realize the ATSDR lists a total of 275 hazardous substances, it becomes clearer than ever just how dangerous this heavy metal can be—especially to the young.

What is this toxic heavy metal doing in a vaccine serum being injected into the bodies of little children in this country? This isn't 1869 or even 1925—we are supposedly technologically advanced. Shouldn't we know better?

POTENTIALLY DEADLY MERCURY EXPOSURE

The United States currently has a very high mass immunization rate. Most people believe that is very good news. Nevertheless, some fear that America children have been exposed to potentially damaging levels of mercury and other toxic materials. Those materials include aluminum and formaldehyde. Formaldehyde is a powerful chemical functioning as the primary component in embalming fluid. It is used to make many building materials such as plywood, and it is used in the manufacture of permanent press clothing, dyes, inks and explosives.

We have all been exposed to potentially dangerous levels of hazardous chemicals. In 1982, the Consumer Product Safety Commission banned the use of foam insulation made with urea-formaldehyde in homes and school buildings. It was considered that formaldehyde vapors from such products were poisonous, even at levels as low as .8 parts per million![7] The National Institute for Occupational Safety and Health (NIOSH) recommends an exposure limit of *0.016 parts per million* for *adults* in the workplace.[8]

What about liquid formaldehyde in childhood injections? Who wants to believe the most serious exposure of all to our kids would come from an *injection of toxins directly into the bloodstream* as part of a government disease-prevention program?

PARENTAL DAVID VS.
GOVERNMENTAL GOLIATH

The FDA finally did something to stop the use of mercury in vaccines in 1998, but only after informed parents began to make their voices heard in Congress and the national media. It took an incredible amount of effort, courage and sheer will power to overcome the medical and governmental "Goliath." The shadow of the giant is still there, however, and ADHD, ADD and autistic spectrum cases continue to flood America's school systems and medical institutions. That is because a great number of mercury-containing vaccines continue to be used in this country.

Toxic metals and chemicals are taking a toll apart from the vaccines. Dr. William G. Crook mentioned a few of the *environmental* hazards playing into the ADHD and hyperactivity problem in the book he wrote with Laura Stevens, *Solving the Puzzle of Your Hard-to-Raise Child:*

> Before the Clean Water Act was enacted in 1972, oceans, rivers and other bodies of water were commonly used as dumping grounds for some of the most toxic substances imaginable, including arsenic, cadmium, mercury, lead, polychlorinated biphenyls (PCBs) and toxic pesticides.[9]

The late Ben F. Feingold, M.D. made this amazing statement about the proliferation of potentially harmful chemicals in 1975 in his landmark book *Why Your Child Is Hyperactive:*

> In 1971, the Stanford Research Institute, under contract to the National Cancer Institute, began work on a system to rank chemicals by their estimated hazard to man. I have been informed by Mr. Arthur McGee, who is in charge of the SRI studies, that since 1839,

when organic chemistry began, *approximately three million chemicals have been synthesized—compounds which never existed in nature.* Of these chemicals, it is estimated that over 30,000 are currently in use for all purposes (industrial, medicinal, agricultural, etc.). Although 5,000 of these compounds have had some tests for carcinogenicity, only 2,000 have been "reliably tested" as to whether they are a cause of cancer.

Of the 30,000 chemicals in use today, over 3,800 occur in our foods as additives. Some of the additives have been studied for carcinogenesis, mutagenesis and blastogenesis, but not a single one of the synthetics used in our food has been subjected to the rigid investigations required for licensing drugs.[10]

Apparently, scientists, vaccine makers and physicians have known about the highly toxic characteristics of mercury and formaldehyde for many decades. Yet they continued to use and dispense relatively high levels of mercury in the form of thimerosal to small children through our nation's compulsory vaccination program. They also use a form of formaldehyde in the production of a number of major vaccines to this day.

Formaldehyde, in the form of "formalin," is a 37 percent solution of gaseous formaldehyde with small amounts of methanol. It "is the chemical of choice to inactivate the viruses used in the production of polio, yellow fever, influenza and hepatitis B vaccines," according to Jamie Murphy, author of *What Every Parent Should Know About Childhood Immunization.*[11]

WHY WORRY ABOUT
A LITTLE CARCINOGEN?

Murphy also said formalin is used to detoxify diphtheria and tetanus toxins, transforming them into "toxoids" in the process. It has been shown to cause allergic reactions, irritation and tumors in humans. In addition, it has produced squamous cell carcinomas (cancers) in the nasal cavities of rats.[12] Although government scientists and medical authorities undoubtedly know about these studies, they don't seem to be worried about "a little carcinogen" being injected into children. Do they know something we don't know?

The only tests I've uncovered for toxicity involved the three *usual* methods of entry into the body—inhalation, skin contact and ingestion. No one seems to have any data for the internal effects of *injected* formalin, but research has shown that an adult will die three hours after ingesting (drinking) just *one ounce* of the stuff.[13]

Perhaps Jamie Murphy offers the best summary of the risks involved with formaldehyde as a component in most of America's childhood vaccines, by asking who…

> …would consider using a hazardous waste, carcinogenic in rats, used in the manufacture of inks, dyes, explosives, wrinkle-proof fabrics, home insulation, and as a major constituent of embalming fluid, and inject it into the delicate body of an infant? What could formaldehyde, aluminum, phenol, mercury, or any number of other deadly chemical substances used in vaccines possibly have to do with preventing disease in children?[14]

WHAT IS A LITTLE FIBROSARCOMA BETWEEN FRIENDS?

Murphy noted that three researchers conducted a study in 1971 to determine the toxicity levels of seven compounds widely used as preservatives or extracting agents for vaccines: Merthioloate (thimerosal), benzethonium chloride, methylparaben, phenol red, pyridine, ethylene glycol and ethylene chlorohydrin.

He writes, "All seven chemicals produced tumors not only at the injection site, but also in other parts of the body...Can there be any doubt that at least three chemicals used in vaccines—thimerosal, benzethonium chloride, and aluminum—are probably causes of induration [hard nodules that appear at the injection site], fibromas [fibrous benign tumors], fibrosarcomas [malignant tumors likely to have a fatal outcome], granulomas, and injection site tumors?"[15]

Some of the other material from which vaccines are made may surprise you according to Leon Chaitow, author of *Vaccination and Immunisation: Dangers, Illusions and Alternatives* (published in Great Britain):

> The material from which vaccines are made is often quite unsettling to contemplate. For example (partial list):
>
> ❏ Diphtheria toxin and antitoxin is derived from putrefying horse blood.
>
> ❏ Pertussis vaccine is taken from mucus from throats of infected children.
>
> ❏ Typhoid vaccine is derived from decomposed fecal material, taken from typhoid victims.
>
> ❏ Salk polio serum was taken from the infected monkeys' kidneys.
>
> ❏ The discredited vaccine, used ineffectively against swine flu, which had such dreadful effects on the recipients, was derived from infected rotten eggs.[16]

ENTER THE OSTRICH AND THE
OFFICIAL BOX OF SAND

As a thinking person, university-trained biochemist and concerned parent, I have to wonder why government officials and key medical leaders continue to ignore these concerns. In my opinion, such clear scientific evidence requires us to rethink our position on the true value of compulsory immunizations in their present state.

An apparent conflict of interest may have a direct effect on what actually happens in this area. Naturally, most medical and governmental leaders want to preserve their reputations and the status quo. Many in the national educational system want to protect the lucrative subsidies local districts receive from government immunization incentive programs. On the other hand, *we want to preserve the lives, health and future of our children.*

Something or someone must "give" in this situation, and the pressure from informed parents and increasingly bold scientific and medical "dissenters" continues to grow. While the official denials mount, the runaway epidemic of ADHD, ADD and autistic spectrum disorders mounts even faster.

This entire debate seems even more risky when you consider just how little it takes to damage or influence the developing nervous systems of growing children. In my mind, it amounts to arguing whether we should give our children just one cup or an entire gallon of unleaded gasoline with their school lunches. This stuff seems unsafe in any amount.

Dr. Feingold described the infinitesimal amount of chemical substance needed to dramatically influence the human nervous system in *Why Your Child Is Hyperactive:*

> So little is known of the nervous system that even conjecture about the mechanism is difficult. However, it is known that a number of natural chemicals in the body

operate on the nervous system. They include serotonin, dopamine, norepinephrine and epinephrine, a
class of substances derived from amino acids and called
biogenic amines...They are considered to be neuro-
transmitters, meaning that they carry impulses at nerve
junctions—from one nerve to another.

[...concerning research to find out what amount of
thyrotropin-releasing factor (TRF) is required to
create activity in the thyroid gland...]

...From this mass of fifty tons [of sheep brain frag-
ments] Dr. Guilleman extracted one milligram of pure
TRF and then found that this product was active and
stimulating at 1 to 5 nanograms, 1 to 5 billionths of a
gram. In the pituitary culture systems, he found that
the product was active at 50 picograms, or 50 trillionths of a gram.

I remain stunned by the exquisitely infinitesimal
amount of activator—stunned that any substance of 50
trillionths of a gram could react in the human body.[17]

If it only takes 50 trillionths of a gram of TRF to affect
the human body, what happens when growing bodies
of American school children are subjected to highly
toxic materials injected into the blood and muscles in
government-mandated vaccinations?

IT ONLY TAKES ONE MOLECULE...

When the Nobel Laureate and eminent Stanford University scientist Linus Pauling was asked what amount of
a compound is required for sensitization in the human
system, he bluntly replied, "A single molecule." As Dr.
Feingold noted, "Molecules vary in size, but a million
small ones can be gathered on a pinhead...*we cannot safely
predict that any part per million or billion or trillion will not
have an effect on certain individuals or on all individuals.*"[18]

The good news is that it is possible to remove harmful heavy metals such as mercury or lead from the human body, a procedure that has produced excellent results in children. If you suspect your child experienced an adverse reaction to a vaccination or has been exposed to harmful substances in another way, then the first step is to determine whether or not your child's body contains dangerous levels of heavy metals or chemicals known to accumulate in body tissues.

Call my office at 1-800-726-1834 for more information about hair sample analysis for mercury, lead, cadmium, arsenic, antimony, etc.

I strongly recommend that you have your child tested for intestinal dysbiosis, or the abnormal function of the intestinal system. This is a particularly common condition among children with ADHD, ADD and autistic spectrum disorder, which leads many to believe it may be a contributing or primary cause of these conditions in some cases.

These conditions often occur or are aggravated by a severe yeast overgrowth in the digestive tract that *should be treated before* any effort is made for mercury detoxification. Even this process may significantly improve or remove many hyperactivity symptoms, according to the research and clinical experience of Dr. William G. Crook and researchers consulting with the Autism Research Institute (ARI), among others.[19]

The Autism Research Institute gathered together twenty-five physicians, chemists, toxicologists and scientists to determine the best way to remove heavy metal contaminants—mercury in particular—from the human body. These medical professionals had treated more than three thousand patients for heavy metal poisoning, including fifteen hundred autistic children. The scientific attendees had a combined total of ninety years of research experience in the toxicology of mercury and other heavy metals.

CHOOSING THE BEST METHOD OF MERCURY DETOXIFICATION

The consensus conference considered nine different detoxification protocols and arrived at a solid consensus or agreement on the best and safest procedure. The ARI has published the official results in a document titled "ARI Mercury Detoxification Consensus Position Paper." This procedure must be done by qualified health professionals. You may contact the ARI directly for more information at 4182 Adams Avenue, San Diego, California 92116, or download the "ARI Mercury Detoxification Consensus Position Paper" at www.autism.com/ari/mercurydetox.html.

Once the dysfunction caused by heavy metals, harmful chemical deposits and yeast overgrowth have been treated in a child's digestive system, nutritional therapies will help the child stay healthy and improve in many areas of behavior and learning ability.

FOLLOW UP WITH VITAMINS

The ARI protocol recommends the supplementation of the following vitamins after the mercury detoxification procedure is complete. This is but a very brief summary of the more detailed recommendations provided in the Defeat Autism Now! (DAN!) Mercury Detoxification Consensus Group Position Paper:[20]

❑ **Vitamin C:** Start daily doses at 5–10 milligrams for every 2.2 pounds of body weight (3–6 IU/2.2 pounds) of buffered or vitamin C esters, and increase to tolerance.

❑ **Vitamin E:** This fat-soluble vitamin can accumulate if given in excess. Dosing in the range of 2–4 milligrams for every 2.2 pounds of body weight every day (3–6 IU/2.2 pounds) is within safe limits.

Mixed tocopherols are the preferred preparation.

❏ **Vitamin B$_6$:** Up to 15 milligrams per every 2.2 pounds of body weight daily of B$_6$ or 3 milligrams for every 2.2 pounds of body weight of pyridoxal-5-phosphate (P5P) to a maximum of 500 milligrams of B$_6$ or 100 milligrams of P5P. (Avoid any preparations that contain supplemental *copper.* Many autistic spectrum children in particular have an excessive amount of copper in their bodies.)

❏ **Alpha-lipoic acid:** This powerful antioxidant may be particularly helpful in autistic children since many of them show evidence of antioxidant depletion. Start with daily doses of alpha-lipoic acid equal to 1–3 milligrams for every 2.2 pounds of body weight and increase to 10 milligrams for every 2.2 pounds as tolerated. This is a natural product of human cells and so has minimal toxicity. (Note: The authors of the ARI consensus paper recommend that this supplement be used only in conjunction with DMSA, which "grabs" or binds to excess mercury released by alpha-lipoic acid.)

❏ **Melatonin:** This pineal hormone helps regulate the sleep/wake cycle and is an antioxidant. Doses of up to 0.1 milligrams per every 2.2 pounds of body weight at bedtime should be adequate, although smaller doses may provide the same benefits. (If your child already has a good sleep cycle, I do *not* recommend supplementation with melatonin.)

❏ **Taurine:** This sulfur-containing amino acid is important in the production of bile salts and, therefore, in the native excretion of toxins and absorption of fats. Many autistic children are deficient in taurine and benefit from a supplementation of 250–500 milligrams per day. A maximum dose of 2 grams per day in adults and adult-sized children is recommended.

❏ **Glutathione:** This is the keystone of the cellular antioxidant system and is often deficient in autistic children. Although people with normal digestive function do not seem to absorb oral doses of this substance, it has clearly helped autistic children. Given the gut dysfunction found in many autistic children, daily doses of oral glutathione at 250–500 milligrams may be of significant help.

Note: The ARI consensus paper also recommends that you *avoid* the following substances due to their suspected interaction with mercury or other heavy metals. Consult with your medical provider before using them: cysteine/cystine, n-acetyl-L-cysteine (NAC), chlorella or other algae.

TEN

Reversing the Dietary Devastation of the Television Generation

While waiting for a flight at the Chicago airport, I saw a seemingly well-educated woman walking toward me with a two-year-old and a four-year-old in tow. I know their ages because I asked the woman after witnessing a fiasco many parents dread.

This mother sat down to feed her children lunch, but both children were screaming; the two-year-old in particular kept breaking away from her. I watched this woman run after the toddler four times in just five minutes (and the older child wasn't behaving much better).

Misbehaving children are a common sight in public places nowadays, but my attention was riveted to the "lunch" the mother was feeding her children. It consisted of some type of spreadable artificial cheese snack food along with a variety of other prepackaged junk foods.

During one of the short intervals when she wasn't chasing her children, the woman received a cell phone call. She was standing close by, and with her distinctively loud voice I couldn't help but overhear her conversation.

Someone had called to talk with her about biopsy reports of some kind. I had to wonder if the lady worked in the medical field. When the cell phone call ended and the mother had retrieved her two-year-old twice more, I asked her, "Are you in the medical field?"

She looked at me inquisitively, so I added, "Please forgive me, but you were standing so close that I couldn't help but overhear you talking about biopsies."

Surprisingly, she dropped her head and said, "No, I'm not in the medical field…the biopsies were for me. I have cancer." The blaring sound of overhead speakers interrupted us as a flight attendant alerted passengers with children to board early, so our conversation ended abruptly. A feeling of sadness came over me as I watched this mother wrestle with her extremely active youngsters and struggle with the information she had just received about her own failing health.

As a nutritionist and biochemist, I felt sadness for two reasons: First, I don't like to see disease strike anyone for any reason. But secondly, I am convinced that many of this mother's problems were caused or amplified—at least in part—by poor dietary choices.

In my view, this well-educated, thirty-something woman appeared to be raising her children on junk food, and they were obviously hyperactive and out of control. Sadly, I see this scenario played out over and over again. Had we talked further, I expect I might have learned that the woman had eaten junk food all of her life. Unfortunately, by raising her children on a diet rich in junk food, unwittingly she was increasing the possibility her children would one day battle cancer as well. Next to accidents, the leading cause of death in children is cancer.

OUR OWN SHAKY FOOTSTEPS

Why does a country with so many affluent and educated people lead the world in per capita cases of attention-deficit hyperactivity disorder, cancer, heart disease and diabetes? Isn't something wrong with this picture? Part of the answer seems obvious: We are training our children to follow in our own shaky footsteps.

A good friend of mine told me about his neighbor who had been diagnosed with ovarian cancer, a lovely mother of four children ranging in ages from two to ten. She was undergoing the standard medical protocol for the disease, which included chemotherapy and radiation. My friend had worked with me on the road for several years and had applied many of the principles and practices I teach about proper dietary choices. He had lost body fat, dramatically increased his energy levels and had eliminated allergy problems. When he talked with his neighbor about changing her personal dietary patterns and those of her children, she came up with several questions she wanted to ask me.

When we met, the first thing I asked her was, "What does your current diet consist of?" It was obvious that she had a wonderful personality, which showed when she laughed and said, "I live on junk food—Twinkies, Ding-Dongs, cupcakes—you name it. If it's junk, I eat it."

I felt a deep sadness in my spirit for this young mother and for her four beautiful children when I heard her response. Predictably, my new acquaintance was unresponsive to my suggestion that she immediately change her diet and that of her children. In due time, this vibrant young mother fell victim to the cancer and died in the prime of her life, leaving the four beautiful children behind.

IF IT'S JUNK…WE ARE INTERESTED!

The truth is that if it's junk, most of the children and young people in America eat it! Those deadly food choices are skillfully imprinted and reinforced by television advertisements devised and filmed by some of the best communicators and persuaders in the world: the men and women in American advertising and entertainment industries.

This pattern of harmful consumption even shows up in our viewing choices for television programming and movies: If it's junk, we watch it...and watch it...and watch it. Day after day, week after week, month after month throughout the years of our lives, we *sit, eat and drink junk while we watch junk*. Meanwhile, muscles atrophy, bones become brittle, joints lose their mobility, and our national health plummets to new lows as our waistlines, cholesterol counts and blood pressures shoot higher and higher. The group most affected by our new fetish with the easy chair is the youth of America.

According to the U.S. Department of Agriculture, more Americans are eating out than ever before. Nearly six out of ten Americans purchased and consumed food away from home each day in 1995, up one-third from 1978. Nearly three out of four teenage males eat at least one meal away from home each day. Nevertheless, researchers say the most apparent increase is specifically among *young children* and females twenty years old and older.

NO SURPRISE

As much as *half* of all our daily calories may be provided (if you can call it that) by the fast foods we choose. Lori G. Borrud, the primary author of the study, said in a speech before the American Public Health Association, "What do we eat when we eat away? The number one choice is beverages, in particular carbonated soft drinks, followed by coffee, then milk. *The favorite soft drink is cola, which comes as no surprise.*"[1] It should come as no surprise that our nation and our young people in particular are in a major health crisis!

The problem actually begins early after birth when many new mothers decide to bottle-feed their babies rather than nurse. My wife, Sharon, has written an excellent book on child nutrition titled *Train Up Your Children in the Way They Should Eat,* and she often teaches classes on the subject. She tells new mothers:

Unless there is a physical reason you cannot nurse your baby, a reason beyond your control, breast-feeding is the best possible way to feed and nourish your child for at least the first nine months of life. It's the best thing for you, too.

Breast milk really is superior to any artificial formula or anything else that you can give your baby. It provides optimal infant nutrition and contains everything that your infant needs. Mother's milk is digested and assimilated better than any formula or any cow's milk you can give your child. Nursing prevents anemia in your baby, and it is also less likely your baby will have any skin disorders if you nurse. There is also a decreased chance of infection and little if any constipation among breast-fed babies. Medical research has established that breast milk contains crucial antibodies that your baby needs during early growth to prepare his or her body for resistance.

The digestive system in a newborn baby is still in the process of developing. A key enzyme necessary for starch digestion isn't even present in an infant's system until he is at least six months of age. That explains why you should not give your baby any cereals or solid food until he is at least six months old.

Cereals are rich in starch, but some babies are fed cereals four to six weeks after birth. The main cause of allergies appears to be linked to feeding infants food they can't digest. Healthy babies are usually nursed exclusively, and receive nothing else for at least six months. If your milk supply is plentiful, it is best to nurse your child for at least twelve to eighteen months.[2]

The importance of breast-feeding cannot be over-emphasized. Researchers have discovered that breast milk and colostrum (the first milk secreted by mothers) do the following:

❏ Inhibit the growth of many bacteria and viruses

❏ Contain numerous antibodies effective against diphtheria, polio virus 1, 2 and 3, mumps, Coxsackie and echo virus, smallpox and influenza organisms [3]

❏ Contain a carbohydrate called bifidus factor, which may encourage the growth of "good" bacteria such as lactobacilli and may prevent the growth of "bad" bacteria such as E. coli bacteria

❏ Prevent intestinal infections and infant diarrhea

❏ Have been proven to neutralize viruses such as polio, herpes simplex, Japanese B encephalitis, St. Louis encephalitis, West Nile, dengue, yellow fever and Western equine encephalitis—even when there was no evidence of corresponding antibodies in the blood serum of the mothers![4]

We already noted in previous discussions about the role vitamin A plays in the healthy development of a child's brain and nervous system. As mentioned, breast-feeding is an infant's most reliable source for this vital vitamin.

I've decided to include an excerpt from Sharon's book specifically for your benefit if you or a family member has an infant in the home. If you start a little one on the right path to good nutrition early, your child will live a longer and happier life.

GOOD SOURCES OF PROTEIN LOW IN FAT AND HIGH IN VALUE

Sharon offers the following recommendations for infant nutrition, excerpted from her book, *Train Up Your Children in the Way They Should Eat.*[5]

Children need a good source of protein every day. Here's a possible scenario for making sure this requirement is met.

❑ *First 3 years:* goat's milk, organic eggs from this point forward

❑ *Ages 4–6:* goat's milk (only if child does not have a weight problem or is not lactose-intolerant), organic eggs, soy protein shakes (call our office for a good source of soy protein)

❑ *Ages 7–8:* high-quality or fresh peanut butter (without partially hydrogenated vegetable oil), soy protein shakes, organic eggs

❑ *Ages 8–12:* clean fish or high-quality organic chicken, soy protein shakes, organic eggs

❑ *Ages 12 and up:* high-quality beef (no more than once a week), soy protein shakes (plus the above)

For children at young ages, meat is not a good answer to the need for protein. Animal protein is very difficult to digest. Avoiding beef altogether is best for your entire family. Even adults with no digestive problems have trouble properly digesting and assimilating animal protein. Our answer has always been "protein shakes."

To begin introducing protein shakes into your child's diet, find out what fruits your child likes. Experiment by making shakes with your child's favorite fruit until she begins asking you for a particular shake. Prepare the shake with high-quality soy protein powder. (Be careful. Some really bad ones exist on the market, even some that are sweetened with aspartame. We choose pure soy protein.) Start your child off slowly with the ingredients so she'll learn to like them. Choose her favorite natural extract and frozen fruit.

Protein shakes provide so much nutrition that starting your child's day with one is a great idea. Toddlers love them. Our oldest son has been drinking protein shakes since he started eating solid foods. We now make enough for all of us to enjoy them after we work out in the gym. Won't you join us?

SUPPLEMENTING YOUR CHILD'S DIET

Why supplements? Today supplementation is a necessity. We are eating more and more processed foods and less and less fresh fruit, vegetables and grains. Our soil is depleted of essential vitamins and minerals, which in turn are lacking in our food. Today we take in more and more pollutants than ever before. It's not the way it was a hundred years ago on great-great-great grandma's and grandpa's farm.

CHILDREN NEED:

❏ Vitamins
❏ Minerals
❏ Protein
❏ Carbohydrates
❏ Fat

YOU CAN PROVIDE VITAMINS, MINERALS, PROTEIN AND FATS FOR INFANTS/TODDLERS WITH THE FOLLOWING:

❏ Goat's milk or mother's milk
❏ Cod liver oil
❏ Flaxseed oil
❏ Liquid or powdered multiple vitamin
❏ Powdered vitamin C

YOU CAN PROVIDE VITAMINS, MINERALS, PROTEIN AND FATS FOR PRESCHOOL CHILDREN WITH THE FOLLOWING:

- ❑ Cod liver oil capsule two to four times a day
- ❑ Flaxseed oil capsule two to four times a day
- ❑ 500 milligrams extra vitamin C powder twice a day
- ❑ Multiple vitamin once a day
- ❑ ½ teaspoon blackstrap molasses once a day (best natural source of iron; can be put in a protein shake)

These supplements can be used as needed (substances marked with "*" are "cold busters"):

- ❑ B complex (only take in the morning since it will increase energy levels)

- ❑ B_6 (affects both physical and mental health; aids in the absorption of vitamin B_{12} in immune system function)

- ❑ *Zinc (promotes healthy immune system and healing of wounds; important in prostate gland function and the growth of the reproductive organs)

- ❑ *Pycnogenol (pine bark extract; a unique flavonol that clinical tests suggest may be as much as fifty times more potent than vitamin E and twenty times more potent than vitamin C in terms of antioxidant activity)

- ❑ Calcium (vital for the formation of strong bones and teeth; tends to have a calming effect on the body; best taken at night for its relaxation qualities)

- ❑ Alfalfa tablets (one of the most mineral-rich foods known to man; roots of the alfalfa plant grow as deep as 130 feet, picking up essential minerals)

- ❏ *Echinacea (stimulates certain white blood cells; good for immune system and lymphatic system)

- ❏ Garlic tablets (or liquid; detoxifies the body and enhances immune system, which protects against infection)

- ❏ Oat bran (extra fiber used in recipes, cereal and protein shake, for example)

- ❏ Unsulfured blackstrap molasses (best natural source of iron)

- ❏ Aloe vera juice (98–99 percent pure aloe vera juice mixed with ⅓ juice helps aid in healing of stomach disorders and colon problems; helps alkalinize an acid system. In general, try to feed your children more alkaline foods and less acidic foods. The foods that are acidic cause the body itself to become acidic, which hinders proper food digestion.)

A special note about vitamin C: Nursing mothers, be sure you are getting plenty of vitamin C in the first three to six months of nursing. If your child is using you as her sole source of food, you will need to be sure that she is getting enough vitamin C from your breast milk. Purchase a high-quality brand of powdered vitamin C.

I have put powdered vitamin C in my oldest son's goat's milk and diluted juice, and he still gets it every day. In fact, our son experiences very few colds. When I notice any early symptoms, I increase his dosage of vitamin C to build up his resistance levels. (If your child's resistance is compromised from lack of sleep or poor diet, he or she will be more susceptible to colds.)

Nursing mothers also need to consume high-quality multiple vitamins. Purchase a high-quality variety, not a synthetic brand that costs you $2.99 at the drug store.

Choosing the right supplements can be very confusing if you don't know what to look for. Remember:

❏ Make sure they come from a reputable source (call our office for information at 800-726-1834).

❏ Children can swallow vitamins sooner than you think. My oldest son started at age two.

❏ Don't give your child an option. It's just like brushing teeth; do you let them have an option on that?

If you have children in your home who are already past the infant stage, you can help protect them from needless health problems tomorrow by controlling the greatest dietary offenders today.

MEET ROBBIE—NEARLY EXPELLED FROM KINDERGARTEN!

My point is perfectly illustrated in the case of Robbie,* the young cousin of one of my colleagues.[6] Robbie was a handsome, bright-eyed youngster with virtually no control over his impulses. His behavior brought him to the brink of expulsion from kindergarten—yes, you read correctly—*kindergarten.*

Robbie's mother took her five-year-old to a pediatrician who referred him to a pediatric psychiatrist. The psychiatrist put Robbie on medication to help calm him and suggested weekly therapy sessions where Robbie would be able to "express himself."

The psychiatrist said he hoped that within a year he would fully understand the five-year-old's psyche and be able to "guide Robbie's consciousness to a full awareness of himself," which would allow Robbie to be at peace.

---

*Not his real name

What a line of rubbish! Robbie is now an adult. He has spent many years in therapy with his behavior largely controlled through medication.

My colleague grew up in a small town where Robbie's grandfather owned a small grocery store. At times he helped people carry groceries to their cars in return for small tips. He said, "I can remember Robbie's mother filling her cart with sugar-sweetened cereals, canned vegetables, processed breakfast tarts, cookies and artificial fruit drinks. Only rarely did fresh fruit or vegetables find their way into the bags that left the store. What is the most amazing to me is that Robbie's family actually believed that they were providing nourishing meals for him."

Sadly, Robbie's mother probably blamed herself or her supposed "lack of parenting skills" for Robbie's misbehavior. On the contrary, his behavior was probably caused by what she was feeding him.

A great deal of research suggests that the parents of "hyperactive" children like Robbie can help to regain control of their children's behavior through some simple choices and dietary and nutritional changes.

In the 1960s and 1970s, Benjamin Feingold, M.D. reported that food additives seemed to be the root cause of hyperactivity in many children. He had found that as many as 40 to 50 percent of the hyperactive children in his studies exhibited a hypersensitivity to food additives such as artificial colors and flavors, preservatives and even some naturally occurring preservatives. He based his claims on over twelve hundred cases in which food additives were positively linked to hyperactivity.

Many attempts were made to refute Dr. Feingold's findings. However, under close scrutiny, their findings reveal some gross flaws.

EVEN SCIENTIFIC RESEARCHERS
EXHIBIT PERSONAL BIAS AT TIMES

In one study, researchers divided hyperactive children into two groups. One group was given one of the items Dr. Feingold claimed would cause hyperactivity, and the second group—supposedly the "control" group—was given a placebo (an inert substance chosen because it would cause no physiological effect). *The placebo in this study was a chocolate chip cookie!* Sugar, chocolate and white flour are all substances that can cause a child to be hyperactive. This "oversight" demonstrated the ignorance and bias many researchers bring with them into their work.

In a second study conducted by the same coordinator of research, children were given 13 milligrams of food dyes twice a day. The scientists released findings saying Dr. Feingold's findings were invalid because 26 milligrams of food dye did not increase hyperactivity in children. The researchers completely missed the fact that *most children consume over 150 milligrams of food dyes daily*, more than five times the dosage used for their so-called research!

Other researchers *confirmed* that 85 percent of the children in their study demonstrated significant learning impairment when administered food dyes at levels of 75, 100 and 150 milligrams daily. Researchers have also demonstrated that severe behavior effects occur even at the 26-milligram level *when food dyes were mixed*, as is the case with most of the prepackaged food products on the typical grocery shelf. [7]

While the majority of studies in the U.S. have not supported Dr. Feingold's claims, scientific reports from other Westernized countries *have*. In fact, some countries have even restricted the use of food additives because of their potential side effects. (You should know that many of the negative studies were funded by food manufacturers and marketing groups in the U.S. These groups share a strong interest in disproving Dr. Feingold's claims.)

Although Dr. Feingold passed away in 1982, his initial theses have been researched, reinforced and refined by such respected physicians and scientists as William R. Crook, M.D., a fellow of the American Academy of Pediatrics and the American College of Allergists and the author of *Help for the Hyperactive Child* (Professional Books, 1991) and *Solving the Puzzle of Your Hard-to-Raise Child* (Random House, 1987).

LIVING WITH YOUR VERY OWN "DR. JEKYLL AND MR. HYDE"?

It is a *fact* that sugar, food dyes and additives exact a high toll on America's school-age children. Consider the case of Jerry, our hypothetical all-American schoolboy. He's feeling a little blue today, and his head is aching. He keeps staring out of the window and hardly pays attention to his teacher.

His teacher doesn't know it, but the Jerry in his class matches the quiet side of the dual-personality central character of Robert Louis Stevenson's classic tale *The Strange Case of Dr. Jekyll and Mr. Hyde*. This teacher knows the calmer "Dr. Jekyll side" of a boy who had his usual breakfast before coming to class today—two doughnuts and a can of soda. In that single soda, Jerry received a significant jolt of caffeine combined with 12 teaspoons of sugar. It is inevitable that Jerry would hit bottom after such intense chemical stimulation. Unfortunately (or fortunately for this particular teacher), the crash came at school just before he entered the classroom.

The teacher in the afternoon class knows a "different" Jerry: the "Mr. Hyde version" riding a chemical high from the sugar cocktail produced by all of the desserts and carbonated sodas he consumed at lunch. Jerry is a behavioral time bomb about to explode, and he is a prime candidate for the label of "ADHD kid" when his hyperactive conduct in the afternoon class lands him in the principal's office once too often.

ELIMINATE PROBLEM FOODS, INVEST IN POWER FOODS

If you already have a dual-natured "Jerry" living in your house who exhibits symptoms of ADD, ADHD or autistic spectrum disorder, I believe you will see immediate improvement if you take several simple steps to *eliminate problem foods*, replace them with *power foods* and provide essential natural vitamins, fatty acids and essential oils to your child's diet.

Sugar is a prime offender in the war on hyperactivity. While a small amount of sugar does not affect healthy children who also eat meals balanced in protein, carbohydrates and fat, it *will create behavioral problems* in children subsisting on a diet filled with processed carbohydrates. Basically, the more sugar such a child consumes, the more restless and destructive his or her behavior becomes.[8]

This truth led researchers to hypothesize that hyperactive children may have a low tolerance to sugar. When scientists conducted glucose tolerance tests on a group of hyperactive children, they found that 75 *percent of those hyperactive children exhibited abnormal results to their glucose tolerance test.*[9]

This means that after the children received the glucose, their body overreacts with excessive secretion of insulin, causing blood sugar levels to actually drop too low. Under these circumstances, the adrenal glands secrete adrenaline to counteract the problem. (When we hear of a sixty-year-old lady who lifts a car off a child, adrenaline is the hormone that enabled her to do that.) So, excess sugar has been shown to increase a child's excitability.

USING AN ELIMINATION DIET

We must not overlook the role of food allergies or sensitivities in ADHD, ADD or autistic spectrum disorders. Some children are more sensitive to food additives than others. Research has also shown many common foods cause sensitivities in children. In a large controlled study, seventy-six severely hyperactive children were treated with an *oligoantigenic diet,* or a diet free of foods that cause hypersensitivity in children. *After only four weeks, 82 percent (sixty-two children) demonstrated significant improvement in their behavior!*

When the offending foods were reintroduced, researchers recorded a dramatic reappearance of hyperactive behavior. The greatest offenders in the study included (ranked in order of sensitivity among the children) red dye (88 percent), yellow dye (80 percent), blue dye (80 percent), coloring and preservative (79 percent) and cow's milk (73 percent).[10]

In my opinion, no caring parent of a supposedly hyperactive or ADHD child can afford to ignore such dramatic research results.

Other factors linked to hyperactivity (or ADHD) and learning disabilities are otitis media (ear infection), nutrient deficiency and exposure to heavy metals. Children with repeated ear infections can experience some hearing loss. These children tend to demonstrate lower scores on standardized tests, such as IQ tests, and can have impaired speech development. Otitis media has also been reported to occur twice as frequently in children with ADD than in children without ADD.[11]

Iron deficiency has also been associated with decreased attentiveness, easy distractibility and decreased voluntary activity.[12] Numerous studies as well as the national media have reported the relationship between learning difficulties and pesticides, dangerous chemicals and heavy metals such as mercury and lead in children's water supply.

(These relationships were examined in detail in the previous chapter.)

WHAT IS A RESPONSIBLE PARENT TO DO?

Begin by eliminating all "high-volatility sugars" from your child's diet. These include more than just white sugar. Eliminate honey, syrup, fruit juices and corn sweeteners such as maltose and dextrose from the diet as well. These sugars essentially react the same as table sugar in the body by raising and then lowering blood sugars as demonstrated in the glucose tolerance test.

Second, eliminate as many artificial food dyes and additives as possible from your child's diet. I would like to tell you to eliminate all of them, but this would be very difficult if not impossible for most of us.

Next I recommend eliminating all the foods listed in this chapter that cause sensitivities in children. After four weeks, you may restore these foods *one at a time* to demonstrate to your satisfaction that they do not contribute directly to your child's hyperactive or ADHD/ADD behavior. (Warning: If your child does become hyperactive, make sure he is not sneaking a Snicker's bar at school before you make your final conclusion!) This is called an *elimination diet*, and it is one of the most useful tools in your arsenal to make life better for a hyperactive or ADHD/ADD child.

Finally, begin to supplement your child's daily diet with vitamins. Studies have shown that some children respond to large doses of B vitamins. One of four hyperactive children in one study demonstrated *significantly improved behavior* when the only change in diet was the addition of a B-vitamin supplement![13] A second study showed that *thirty-two of thirty-three* children responded to doses of 1.5–6 grams of niacin, taken with 3 grams of vitamin C. After the trial, all were removed from the supplementation, and every child relapsed within thirty days.[14]

"VITAMIN" PRODUCTS THAT MAY MAKE THINGS WORSE!

I must stress that just because the label on a jar or package says "vitamins" does not mean its contents will help your child. The truth is that some so-called "vitamin" products may even make your child's problem worse. Many children's vitamin preparations are laced with sugar, artificial flavors and artificial colors—some of the very things you want your ADHD/ADD or autistic-spectrum child to avoid!

Manufacturers often extract B vitamins from yeast, which itself often causes sensitivities in children and adults. Make sure your B vitamin has a rice base that is free of any chemicals that may make your child's symptoms worse. (Contact our office for information about supplement products that have been tested and proven to be the very best for you and your family. We can also provide information on noninvasive testing to help you detect even low-grade levels of heavy metal [lead or mercury] toxicity and mineral deficiencies.)

If you are at your wits' end with your child's behavior, consider the evidence presented in this chapter. Extensive research suggests that what you put into your child's mouth may determine what you are able to put into his head.

I have prepared an outline with dietary and nutritional instructions based upon my clinical observations after working with thousands of patients on a one-on-one basis. Frankly, most of what I have learned was not taught to me in graduate school. My suggestion is that you follow this program as outlined. I believe that you will have excellent results.

If your child is currently taking prescription medications, always consult with your physician or a nutrition-minded physician before you begin this program or discontinue any medication.

RECOMMENDED EATING PROGRAM

This program has produced seemingly incredible results in the lives and behavior of many children labeled with ADHD, ADD and autistic spectrum disorders. While I make no claims that these measures constitute a "cure" for these conditions, they have helped many people. Try these recommendations for four weeks, and I believe that you will be pleased with the results! I am convinced the positive results will be all the reinforcement you will need to have your child remain on this program.

❑ *No dairy products.* All dairy products must be eliminated. This includes milk, cheese, ice cream and yogurt. *This is the single most important restriction!*

❑ *No junk food.* If it comes in a cellophane wrapper, throw it away.

❑ *No yellow foods.* Most important here are corn and squash. Children with ADHD/ADD and autistic spectrum disorders are commonly hypersensitive to these types of food.

❑ *No fruit juices.* Fruit juice is a very concentrated source of sugar and sometimes can contain more sugars than soda. (One glass of apple juice contains up to 8 teaspoons of sugar!) Eat the fruit instead. It has more fiber and vitamins.

❑ *No hydrogenated oils.* This includes margarine, vegetable shortening (no matter how famous the brand) and the thousands of products—such as brand-name peanut butter products—that contain them. *READ THE LABEL!* If the ingredients say hydrogenated or partly hydrogenated oil, *leave it on the shelf!* The hydrogenation process is done to make the oil remain "hard" at room temperature.

It also remains "hard" in your arteries!

❑ *Cut sugar intake by 95 percent.* Once again, read the labels and get it out of the diet!

❑ *Eliminate chocolate.* Also, eliminate any source of caffeine.

❑ *No aspartame, Equal or NutraSweet products.* Try Barley Malt Sweetener instead. It is available at quality health food stores, it isn't very expensive, and it is an all-natural product.

❑ *No processed meats.* This includes most meats purchased in the deli case. The offending chemical ingredients—sodium nitrite and sodium nitrate—are known cancer-causing agents (carcinogens). Leave it alone if it has MSG (monosodium glutamate), too. Even if these ingredients are absent, *never eat pork or shellfish.* These scavenger species of land and sea are known to "filter" wastes and retain toxic substances in the very body tissues that seem so attractive to our taste buds. (Read my book *Maximum Energy* for detailed information about the pros and cons of pork products and shellfish.[15])

❑ *Improve breakfast—serve moderate protein, moderate complex carbohydrate meals.* Eliminate breakfast cereals with milk. For lunch and dinner, serve fresh meals consisting of about 40 percent protein and 60 percent complex carbohydrates. Remember, too much protein causes a net decrease of body calcium stores and contributes to heart disease and possibly cancer.

❑ *Eat fresh fruits and vegetables as much as possible!*

❑ *Use specific vitamin supplements:*

❑ *Metagenics brand multivitamin.* This is a hypoallergenic multivitamin that is better absorbed in the digestive system. It does not contain the dyes and chemicals often found in other best-selling multivitamins (again, these ingredients have been shown to aggravate symptoms of ADHD/ADD and autistic spectrum disorders).

❑ *Vitamin C.* Choose a powdered form of vitamin C ascorbate that is pH-neutralized. This will not make the body acidic as other types may.

❑ *Protein supplements.* Be sure the protein is not extracted from dairy sources. We recommend a product developed by Nutrition and Medical Research Labs, which is available through our office.

❑ *Zinc, calcium citrate and magnesium chloride.* (Note: Please use only as directed on the label.)

❑ *Flaxseed oil and/or primrose oil.* These Omega-3 essential fatty acids will be an excellent aid for the ADHD/ADD and autistic spectrum child. I recommend that each member of the family over age six take two capsules of each daily. (All children need these!)

❑ *Vitamin E.* Take 100 international units (IU) daily.

❑ *Chromium picolinate.* This element enhances the metabolic effects of the insulin your body manufactures each day.

❑ *Vanadyl sulfate.* This element promotes glucose transport across the cell membrane, making cellular energy transfer more efficient. It can also reduce sugar cravings.

If you choose to eat junk food as an adult, it is your decision. However, I urge you to remember that your child's health is greatly determined by what he or she eats during these tender, developmental years. Please, for the sake of your children, teach them to choose healthy food alternatives today for a healthy tomorrow. To help you in this, you can call my office at (800) 726-1834 and order a copy of my *Eat, Drink & Be Healthy* program.

ELEVEN

Keys to Proper Parental Control: Consistency, Caring and Compassion

There is a nationwide crisis in the area of parental discipline, again a product of our "no-boundaries, no morals" generation. This has drastically affected several generations of children at this writing, and nowhere is this more apparent than in the nation's public schools. One documentary video, "Crisis in the Classroom" hosted by Phyllis Schafly, stated:

> Several studies, including a 1993 *USA Today* survey of 65,000 students...found that 37 percent do not feel safe in school. Nearly half of all male students had been hit or struck during the previous school year. More than half knew that weapons were carried to school regularly, and 43 percent of all public school students avoided the restrooms out of fear of harm.
>
> In response, schools have spent millions of dollars on crime prevention, but violent crime continues to escalate. At least three million serious crimes were committed in public schools last year, including more than 465,000 violent assaults. At least 5,000 public school teachers are attacked every month. Many

believe the increase in public school crime is a reflection of changed attitudes toward student discipline.[1]

It seems clear to me that America's crisis in the classroom begins, in many cases, with the crisis in America's living rooms. Ask yourself how many thirteen-year-olds you know who are polite. Without getting specific, how many of them act like unbelievable brats who won't even speak to you or glance in your direction when you ask them a question?

This is clearly a difficult time in human development with hormonal overdrive combined with incredible mental potential unleashed together, yet previous generations seemed to bridge the gap with relative grace and stability. There is very little grace or stability in many of today's American families, but it is far easier to fix these problems at home than in the teeming social fishpond of a public school setting.

In previous chapters, extensive scientific documentation was often the rule. We will draw from a different and far more credible well in this chapter—time-proven principles with the added wisdom of multiple generations of parental experience.

Behavioral psychologists, psychiatrists and others have conducted a great deal of research in this area, but much of what they propose is based upon behavior modification studies of rats and dogs and is largely predicated upon concepts totally opposite from time-tested traditions.

Most of the "pop-psychology parenting" ideas that swept through society over the last fifty years also contradicted the common wisdom held throughout history by every major culture and civilization. The mess in our public school system presents a troubling microcosm of the "harvest" society is reaping from such rebellious seeds.

THE THREE-PART FOUNDATION
OF PROPER PARENTAL DISCIPLINE

I use three words to describe the foundation of proper parental discipline and child-rearing: *consistency*, *caring* and *compassion*.

These things apply to the training of all children, but those labeled as ADD or ADHD especially benefit from proper parental training, discipline and control. Where children with symptoms of ADHD, ADD or autistic spectrum disorders are concerned, parents may see limited results if the underlying physiological or biochemical problems described in previous chapters aren't eliminated. However, once these problems are removed or minimized, *proper training, discipline and control become crucial life components for success in life.* The goal is straightforward: to raise self-disciplined, caring and compassionate children who will succeed in their life goals to their fullest potential.

"CAN I GIVE HIM BACK?"

This goal sounds noble, but the reality is that parenting isn't easy! The picture of a cooing baby contentedly gurgling and smiling at adoring parents is wonderful—it's the next two decades of child-rearing that make so many parents want to show up at the hospital to say, "Can I give this child back?"

One time we sold Baron, who was a registered Alaskan malamute, to a woman who just had to have him. We'd only had Baron for about a year, but we traveled so much at the time that we decided to sell him. When the lady arrived, I said, "Let me explain something to you about Baron. When he was a puppy, he was attacked and scratched by a large cat. He really, *really* dislikes cats. Since he weighs about 130 pounds, it should be obvious that cats don't have much of a chance if he catches them. Do you have any other pets?"

The lady said, "Oh, I've got three cats."

I replied, "Well, I highly suggest to you that you don't buy Baron—especially if you plan to keep him in your house along with your three cats."

"Oh no, I've got other dogs," she said. "My cats get along with all my other dogs. My dogs and cats have no problem getting along."

I felt honor bound to say, "Yes, but you should remember that malamutes are predators. They were originally used as hunting dogs. Besides, Baron doesn't like cats. Honestly, I think you're going to have a problem if you buy him."

The lady just shook her head and said, "Oh no, I want him. This dog is absolutely beautiful—we have to have this dog."

I said, "OK, fine, no problem," and they took Baron home on a Friday.

The following Monday they called me back and said, "Can we bring Baron back?"

"What's the matter?"

After releasing a deep sigh, the lady said, "I can't believe this. For the past three days Baron has terrorized the cats of the house. They've lived on top of the drapes. They cling to the top of the curtains and hang on the curtain rods. They are so scared that they won't come down. They're terrified, and all Baron does is jump on the wall and try to kill the cats."

I said, "Well, I warned you that Baron doesn't like cats."

"We know, but we want to bring him back."

"IS THIS THE CUSTOMER SERVICE COUNTER?"

How many parents find themselves in the same situation? They rejoice when a child first enters their lives, but after six or eight months of screaming, colic, mountains of diapers and back-to-back sleepless nights, they may be tempted at times to think, *I wonder if we can take this child back?* The same thing happens when the child reaches six or seven years of age and gets in trouble at school for being defiant and refusing to listen: "Can we take this child back?" The truth is that there is no "customer service counter" for frustrated parents.

It doesn't have to be this way. Yes, you will face challenges, hard work and radically altered priorities, but children *are* a blessing from God. His Word is filled with proven advice to help you raise your children properly. Perhaps the most appropriate scripture is found in Proverbs 22:6: "Train up a child in the way he should go, and when he is old he will not depart from it."

CONSISTENCY

One of the primary jobs of the parent is to set boundaries for right behavior, safety and godly living. The very task of setting boundaries is difficult enough, but consistently enforcing and reinforcing them is even harder. The good news is that the good benefits of parental labors last a lifetime.

Anytime boundaries are created for human behavior, then the *consequences* for crossing or defying those boundaries are not far behind. When we tell little Johnny or Jenny not to run out into the street, the consequences of his or her disobedience could easily be death.

It is the parent's responsibility to teach and reinforce this parental boundary early and in safe ways *before* the child faces a situation with such a severe consequence. Two concepts and two principles are linked to the process of correction and training. According to Gary and Ann Marie Ezzo's *Growing Kids God's Way: Biblical Ethics for Parenting:*

> *Punishment* is the fitting retribution of an offense. In child training, it serves a moral purpose; it communicates to children a value of good and evil by the weight of punishment ascribed to each wrongful act. The

administration of punishment is dependent upon and inseparably linked to the proper administration of authority…

Punishment employs correction, but not all correction is associated with punishment. *Correction* is the act of bringing back from error or unacceptable deviation from the standard.[2]

The Ezzos also offer two "rules of correction" wise parents should observe: 1) The type of correction depends on the presence or absence of evil motive, and 2) the punishment/consequence must fit the crime.[3]

The effectiveness of parental authority disintegrates every time we fail to be consistent. Many parents *threaten to punish* over and over, but their children are too smart to fall for empty threats. They put more weight in *experience* than in verbal propositions.

"NOW I'M REALLY GOING TO SPANK YOU"

One time a friend and her five-year-old son joined another family for a motor home trip. The father of the host family listened to his friend tell her son (as many as fifteen or twenty times!), "If you do this again, I'm going to spank you! Now I'm going to spank you…I'm *really* going to spank you. That's it—I'm going to spank you." Yet she never followed through, and that little five-year-old continued to misbehave openly and continuously in the motor home.

Later on, the boy's mother left him with her host so she could play some basketball with the man's son (who was older). Unmoved by his mother's absence or stern warnings of wrath to come before she left, this young guest proceeded to misbehave right in front of his host. This time it was his turn, so he said, "Young man, if you do this again, I'm going to spank you on the bottom."

Naturally, the five-year-old looked at the man and boldly committed his crime again.

Without delay or further warnings, the man picked him up and popped him on the bottom with a ping-pong paddle. The boy immediately looked at the man in shock and started crying. With a gentle voice the host father said, "Let me tell you something, son. Every time I tell you that I'm going to spank you, you are going to get spanked immediately. You won't get a second chance. When I tell you you're going to get spanked, you're going to get spanked." Needless to say, this man didn't have another problem with his young guest, and the boy's mother was amazed at the mysterious "transformation" in her son.

My wife and I developed our own ways of dealing with our children. We taught our oldest son that whenever we said *g'nuck*, a German word that basically means "enough," then we would discipline him in private if he continued his incorrect behavior.

CHILDREN WON'T DIE
IF YOU SPANK THEM

Some people who have heard me talk about this have told me, "I can't believe you condone being mean to children by popping them with a paddle." The Bible tells us:

> Don't fail to correct your children. They won't die if you spank them. Physical discipline may well save them from death. My child, how I will rejoice if you become wise. Yes, my heart will thrill when you speak what is right and just. Don't envy sinners, but always continue to fear the LORD. For surely you have a future ahead of you; your hope will not be disappointed. My child, listen and be wise. Keep your heart on the right course.
>
> —Proverbs 23:13–19, NLT

God certainly does not advocate child abuse, but He does speak of the proper way to discipline in the Scriptures. There is a proper way to discipline, but child abuse is wrong, and it is illegal. No parent should *ever* physically harm a child by bruising or leaving marks on his body. However, an occasional swat on the bottom sure doesn't hurt a child, especially a child who simply doesn't want to listen.

Even older children need discipline in some form. No matter how old your child may be, he still needs to know that there is going to be discipline of some kind involved in the household. You may feel spanking is no longer an option in your child's teen years, but you should still establish clear consequences for wrong actions and follow through *consistently*.

CHILDREN RESPECT STRENGTH

Psychologist James Dobson, founder and president of Focus on the Family, made some excellent observations about children and consistent, determined discipline in his book *The Strong-Willed Child*:

> But why are children so pugnacious? Everyone knows that they are lovers of justice and law and order and secure boundaries. The writer of the book of Hebrews in the Bible even said that an undisciplined child feels like an illegitimate son or daughter, not even belonging to his family. Why, then, can't parents resolve all conflicts by the use of gentle pats on the head? The answer is found in this curious value system of children, which respects strength and courage (when combined with love)…
>
> When a parent refuses to accept his child's defiant challenge, *something changes in their relationship*. The youngster begins to look at his mother and father with disrespect; they are unworthy of his allegiance. More

important, he wonders why they would let him do such harmful things if they really loved him. The ultimate paradox of childhood is that boys and girls *want* to be led by their parents, but insist that their mothers and fathers *earn the right to lead them.*[4]

CARING AND COMPASSION

It takes attention, determination, concentration and old-fashioned courage to raise children in our modern culture—and *double* that for parents of children labeled with ADHD, ADD or autistic spectrum disorder. Even more, effective parenting requires large doses of *caring* and *compassion*. These are the components of love that direct, empower and set boundaries for the proper administration of discipline when it is needed.

While some parents blindly punish their children for all offenses regardless of circumstances, wiser parents take great care to separate real acts of disobedience and disrespect from minor acts of forgetfulness, childishness or actions beyond their personal control.

Particularly for parents of children with symptoms of ADHD, ADD or autistic spectrum disorders, the first task is to *separate* actions or compulsions related to the specific problems that are hindering their lives. If your child is uncontrollably hyperactive due to diet, then change the diet. If you suspect food allergies or food dyes, then begin to conduct a controlled elimination diet to isolate the offending substances and remove them from the diet.

If none of these measures work, you may feel that a physical or biochemical factor may be involved (such as a lack of vitamin A). Do your research, consult with trusted health professionals, and see if you can find the solution.

Many parents of children diagnosed with autistic spectrum disorders must face serious behavioral, social and learning disabilities in their children. These children require even more love and constant maintenance each day, and parents must take extra care not to punish a child for behaviors or "compulsions" beyond the child's control. However, there are some very effective programs available to help teach these children how to overcome some of the compulsivity of the disorder and increase their ability to focus and function better in everyday skills. [5]

SPECIAL-NEEDS CHILDREN NEED APPROPRIATE DISCIPLINE

Again, children with special health and behavioral problems should *never* be punished for actions beyond their control, but they *do* benefit from appropriate parental discipline for wrong behavior *within* their control. In my view, the parents are the best judges of proper discipline methods and guidelines for their own children.

Unlike a computer program that "runs on its own" once it is loaded, the parenting program requires constant diligence and effort for success. Every day presents you with difficult decisions and choices. Did Johnny fail to clean up his room because of a normal childish lapse in memory or sudden distraction, or was it a calculated disobedience meant to challenge authority? The answer to such questions has everything to do with proper consequences and the exercise of parental authority.

It is crucial for parents to remember that certain behavioral patterns are built into certain children. Socrates, the Greek philosopher, noticed that people seemed to fall into four general personality types or temperaments:

❑ *Melancholic* (generally "down" or depressed, the "glass is half empty" view of life, often seen in artistic people)

❑ *Phlegmatic* (generally impassive, easy-going with a cold or calm fortitude)

❏ *Sanguine* (sturdy, high color, cheerful, "the glass is half full" view)

❏ *Choleric* (passionate, easily moved to anger, quick-tempered)

Although I disagree with many of this early philosopher's teachings, I believe this particular observation at the very least highlights the fact that God made each of us unique individuals who are, by design, different from one another in specific ways—even within the same family.

For instance, I am what some behavioral psychologists would call a "Type A" personality. I am a driver; it has been my instinct to take a leadership role throughout my life. I am almost driven to do the best I possibly can with everything that I do, and I often find it difficult to understand why everyone doesn't approach life the same way I do. In general, these basic motivations are ingrained in my nature, and they can't really be changed without changing who I am. This doesn't excuse me from obeying the law, being courteous to others or working with others in a team effort when necessary. Still, the fact is that God created me with a basic foundation of characteristics that form my personality.

HARNESSING THE STRENGTH OF THE WILL

Dr. James Dobson did an excellent job of describing the different characteristics of human character he saw even from the moment of birth:

> Another newborn characteristic is most interesting to me and relates to a feature which can be called "strength of the will." Some children seem to be born with an easygoing, compliant attitude toward external authority...

Just as surely as some children are naturally compliant, there are others who seem to be defiant upon exit from the womb. They come into the world smoking a cigar and yelling about the temperature in the delivery room and the incompetence of the nursing staff and the way things are run by the administrator of the hospital. They expect meals to be served the instant they are ordered, and they demand every moment of mother's time.[6]

To force a child who is very amiable, or phlegmatic as Socrates would say, into a high-pressure leadership role may directly conflict with that child's temperament. However, many people seem to possess a "mix" of these personality types. We have seen presidents who were strong leaders but who also possessed enough "phlegmatic" characteristics to get along with people from many different political backgrounds in times of war or crisis.

If a child is basically a melancholy who likes to make detailed charts and organize things, it is basically wrong (or impossible) to force him to be a sanguine who is very lively and spirited.

DON'T TRY TO CHANGE YOUR CHILD'S BASIC TEMPERAMENT

Wise parents carefully observe their children and do everything they can to foster the God-given talents and desires they received at birth. It is unwise for anyone to try and change the basic temperament of a child. (Again, I am not talking about "going with the flow" of a lawless or rebellious streak in a child—we are still reaping four decades of that kind of nonsense.)

My son Harrison drove this point home in a way I will *never* forget. Harrison is also a "Type A" personality. In fact, his little personality almost exactly matches mine. (I hope the world is ready for him.) Very often, I will shut myself in my bedroom so I can do an early morning radio talk show over the telephone—without interruptions.

One day I was at home in Florida, in the middle of a live radio broadcast airing out of Portland, Oregon, from the privacy of my bedroom when Harrison decided he needed to talk to Daddy.

Harrison was only twenty-four months old at the time, so he neither understood nor cared that I was doing a live radio show being heard by potentially millions of people. All this little "Type A" toddler knew was, *I want to talk to Daddy.* On the other hand, I couldn't understand a thing he was saying either because he was still talking baby talk.

When Harrison entered the room and started talking to me, I tried to roll over to the other side of the bed with the phone in my hand. He quickly climbed up on the bed and onto my shoulders. Then he wanted to see what I was doing with the phone. Fortunately, the radio station went to a commercial break so I jumped up, laid down the phone receiver, and ran into the bathroom where we had another phone installed. This would have worked except for two problems: 1) It was just a sliding door called a "pocket door," and 2) a very determined "Type A" toddler was on the other side.

TRAPPED IN A TOILET BY A TWO-YEAR-OLD!

Harrison wasn't about to give up. He grabbed the sliding door and started yelling for Daddy. By this time, I was back on the air talking live to listeners. The only place to sit in the room was on the toilet, so there I was, looking at my determined toddler and thinking, *This is unbelievable. He won't quit yelling, and I can't say anything to him because I'm sitting on a toilet trying to do a live radio broadcast.*

Then I remembered the linen closet situated right beside the bathroom. I opened the linen closet with one hand, held the phone with the other and tried unsuccessfully to squeeze my body into the small space. In desperation, I hooked the back of the closet door with my right foot and pulled it in as much as I could. Then I stuck my head in between the sheets, pillows and towels and maneuvered the phone receiver close to my mouth hoping to mute the sound of Harrison's increasingly insistent cries.

It must have been a hilarious picture. There I was, a forty-five-year-old man cornered by his tiny "Type A" two-year-old who was yelling for Daddy and pulling on the door of a small linen closet. Meanwhile I was desperately holding the door with my foot while conducting a live radio talk show via telephone in a state on the other side of the continent.

NOW WHAT AM I GOING TO DO?

Frankly, this incident was one of the funniest things that I've ever experienced. At the time, however, I thought, *This is ridiculous; now what am I going to do?* I knew it was simply Harrison's nature to seek out his daddy, so there was no reason to discipline him over the incident. I knew Harrison really didn't understand what he was doing, so I told him, "Harrison, when Daddy is on the phone, it's really impor-tant that you don't talk to me and that you let me talk on the phone to whomever I'm talking."

In retrospect, it is obvious to me that since Harrison was two, he didn't know what a phone was and that there was somebody else on the other end of the phone line. He just wanted to spend time with Daddy.

It is very important to set clear limits for your children ahead of time, and then to make sure you maintain those limits consistently. Be sure you control any anger or emo-tional release before you discipline your children, and never belittle or berate them. Instruction, correction and punishment should deal with specific acts of disobedience and underlying motives, not the innate value of a child. As parents, we should love our children unconditionally in the same way that God loves us, whether we are "sinners or saints," while also holding us ultimately responsible for our personal decisions and actions.

Sometimes we undercut the primary goal in the process of overreacting to a specific situation. Any parent will verify the tendency of children to "hide the evidence" of their wrongdoings from time to time, but these incidents often offer ideal opportunities to teach them that "honesty pays." In other words, if your child "hides the evidence" of his wrongdoing but later comes to you and tells the truth about the incident, make sure you don't overreact and thus teach them *never to confide to you or other adults again*. In this situation, truthful confession makes mercy more effective than "justice."

REINFORCE THE GOOD, DISCOURAGE THE BAD

If you discipline a child after she tells the truth, she may gradually lose faith in you and stop telling you the truth. If the wrong still deserves some kind of discipline, devise a significantly lesser punishment and make it clear you are showing her mercy *because* she told you the truth. Good parenting always reinforces the good and discourages the bad.

One of the primary purposes of godly parental discipline is to help children *listen* and *focus their attention* upon instruction or correction. Sometimes you must tailor discipline for each individual child.

Years ago my family visited Yellowstone National Park in the Teton Range in Wyoming during the winter. We decided to go dogsledding with another family through Yellowstone, complete with sleds, sled dogs and an experienced dogsledder to help us "mush" correctly. I'll never forget the experience of watching the sled dog pull that sled loaded with Sharon and Austin bundled up under the blankets while I ran along behind or stepped up on the back skid with the driver or "musher." Our sled moved along at a rate of eight or ten miles per hour until the dog pulling the sled ahead of us suddenly decided he wouldn't listen to the musher.

The dogsledder promptly stopped the sled, ran up to the dog, threw him down and bit him on the ear! I couldn't believe that I was watching what I felt was an act of barbarity. The dog was howling because the guy actually drew blood.

"What in the world are you doing?" I asked.

The experienced dogsledder calmly explained, "Well, the dog wouldn't listen. He wouldn't pull because he wasn't paying attention and wasn't focused. I kept telling him to do something, and he wouldn't listen."

"Well, why did you bite him?" I asked.

When he said, "Well, that's how the mother dog administers correction," I suddenly understood the man's motivation. What appeared to be a barbarous act to me was actually this man's effort to match the dog's "crime" with the appropriate "dog punishment." I've heard of a similar technique in which American Plains Indians used to slide up on a horse's neck to bite its ear to tame or train a wild and unbroken horse.

PROPER CORRECTION
INCREASES FOCUS AND ATTENTION

While I would never encourage you to "bite your child on the ear," I am saying that proper correction requires you to help your child focus and pay attention. When my sons display a lack of focus and inattention, I give them a gentle squeeze in a spot between the edge of the shoulder and the neck where a muscle called the "trapezius muscle" is located. The area is very sensitive, so pain isn't needed—just a slight squeeze will immediately regain a child's attention. When you say, "OK, now listen to me," and squeeze the trapezius muscle, even the most disinterested boy will say, "Yes, Dad, yes sir."

RESPECT DOESN'T COME BY ACCIDENT

Many of the adults who emerged from the 1960s and 1970s can't believe I teach my children to say "Yes sir" and "No ma'am." The problem is that if you don't teach them to respect authority and one another, then they won't. Respect is a concept best taught by example. It never seems to happen by accident or by "passive osmosis."

William J. Bennett, a fellow speaker with whom I've done many seminars and the former U.S. Secretary of Education, wrote in the introduction to his book *The Book of Virtues: A Treasury of Great Moral Stories:*

> Moral education—the training of heart and mind toward the good—involves many things. It involves rules and precepts—the *dos* and *don'ts* of life with others—as well as explicit instruction, exhortation and training. Moral education must provide training in good habits. Aristotle wrote that good habits formed at youth make all the difference. And moral education must affirm the central importance of moral example. For children to take morality seriously they *must* be in the presence of adults who take morality seriously.[7]

In the long term, children who never learn to respect authority or how to publicly demonstrate respect for others disqualify themselves for any form of public service, international commerce, foreign relations work or well-paying jobs involving people.

In most of our nation's public schools, you might be surprised by the response you would get from many of our eight-, nine- and ten-year-old students if you asked them a question in the hallway. A few would even make a vulgar gesture before turning their back on you. A good number might simply ignore you or answer "Yeah?" at best.

Children who have never been taught respect will rarely if ever show respect. Again, this is the product of the failed and bankrupt ideas of the rebellious 1960s, and its heritage of failure has been passed on from generation to generation.

MOM: "THANK YOU; PLEASE SPANK HIM MORE"

These children generally have no respect for you or for themselves because they don't know what their limits are. That is why I believe in a strong disciplinary action if a child does not say "Yes sir" or "No sir," whether it means you put them in the corner or pop them on the bottom with a paddle.[8]

When I managed to earn a well-deserved spanking in fifth or sixth grade, at first I used to go home and tell my mother. But I stopped doing that almost immediately because she would call the principal and say, "Thank you; please spank him more."

A former school principal lives next to my offices, and he said he still remembers the days when the parents would call to thank him for spanking their children. They noticed a clear difference in the behavior and manner of their children.

Today, school principals and administrators risk an instant lawsuit if they spank a child, but I think we've lost something along the way. Children need discipline, and the reality is that they really don't need to be spanked all the time. The only kids who get constant correction are those who never "get the point" in the first place. Many teachers complain that they expend so much time trying to control the classroom with ineffective techniques today that they don't have time to teach.

DELIVER TEN TIMES
MORE LOVE THAN DISCIPLINE

If you choose to use corporal or physical punishment in the discipline of your child, I want to remind you to give him ten times more love than discipline. Discipline is only effective when it is administered out of genuine love and concern for a child's well-being. In my home, discipline is reserved for three serious behaviors or outcomes: disobedience, disrespect and bad grades. Many people question the third category, but I'm convinced it should be included. A child has a great deal of advance warning in this area, and as long as the grade standard is geared to the child's actual potential, it is fair. Poor grades have a *direct effect* on a child's prospects for success and fulfillment as an adult.

Any child who goes to college thinking Cs are acceptable will never get into the graduate school of his choice (if he even gets into graduate school). Average grades are not acceptable for any child who wants to go into a "white collar" or skilled occupation, plans to attend graduate school or dreams of becoming a medical doctor, a dentist, a lawyer or any other advanced occupation.

Consider enrolling your child in extracurricular activities that increase personal discipline and tend to reinforce the principles you teach in your home. That may include a Scout program, gymnastics, dance, music lessons or a well-run martial arts program.

I enrolled my oldest son in a karate program, and he holds a black belt in karate at the age of thirteen. He has a good attitude, demonstrates respect for his elders and is extremely disciplined in his personal, social and spiritual life. He isn't perfect (who is?), but he is a fine son who makes his father proud. The training paid an unexpected dividend as well recently when some boys decided they would beat him up in a church parking lot. They misjudged my son because he was quiet, well behaved and polite to adults. They challenged him and tried to attack him, but within a matter of seconds he had the situation under firm control, and the confrontation was over.

In that moment, my son realized why I had him taking karate for four years. When a challenge came, he took care of it quietly and quickly and emerged from the test with even more self-esteem.

When he turns sixteen years old, my son will start junior college. By the age of eighteen, he will have already completed basic courses such as physics, math, calculus and organic chemistry so he can move directly into advanced studies at the university level when he knows what he wants to do.

MAKE INTENTIONAL CHANGES FOR INTENTIONAL RESULTS

As parents, one of the most valuable things we can do is teach our children how to make intentional changes in life for intentional results. We must teach them early that they are responsible for their own choices and investments in life.

If you have a child who has a lot of health problems, but you don't find the causes and change his diet or lifestyle choices, your child will probably suffer from those same health problems when he or she grows into adulthood. If your child has a problem with socialization skills, help him change what he's doing so he won't be hindered by the same problem as an adult.

Train your children to be the *exceptions*, the disciplined risktakers, the determined producers, the visionary builders, the ones who come through when others fall away. Sow success into them as children, and they will reap a harvest of success as adults. It has been incorrectly said that "it takes a village" to raise a child. I would say that it only takes one child raised as a winner to bless an entire nation.

In the spring of 2001, I took my family on a national book promotion tour in our motor home. While driving through a rural area of Pennsylvania, we saw a billboard advertising the shopping opportunities in this particular town, and we decided to take a break of see the sights.

IT ONLY TAKES ONE *"MOVER AND SHAKER"*

The weather was cold, and to our surprise we couldn't find any shops in this little town. Finally, I noticed a man standing out in front of a repair shop that had gone out of business, and I pulled into his parking lot.

"Sir," I said, "where is all the shopping in this town?"

He said, "Oh, all the shopping closed about three years ago."

"What do you mean it closed?" I asked.

He looked closely at me, shook his head and said, "Well, you know, we had us a real mover and shaker back then. You know it only takes one of those."

Sharon and I started laughing, and I turned off the engine of our motor home off. "What do you mean?" I said.

"Well, when you get one mover or shaker, they can really change the community," he said. "Our town is over one hundred years old, and I mean this lady had people coming from all over the country in buses just to visit us and buy things from our shops—we had shops everywhere. Then her husband got transferred over to Philadelphia, and everything just kind of closed up. Naturally, she had to go with him, so now we're just kind of back to where we were."

Then the man looked at me and nodded toward the road. "Matter of fact," he said, "If you want to get this bus back over to the highway, then you need to go back the way you came. That road gets real narrow going this way, and I don't think you can get through these roads."

I told Sharon, "Isn't it interesting that *it only takes one mover or shaker to get things changed.*" It only took one Rosa Parks to refuse to sit "at the back of the bus" to launch the social revolution we call the Civil Rights Movement. It only took one determined preacher like Dr. Martin Luther King, Jr. to lead the Civil Rights Movement to the door of the power brokers in Washington, D.C.

It is amazing to see what one mover and shaker can do in the world. That is why it is so important that we do our best to be movers and shakers in our generation, and to teach and discipline our children to become tomorrow's movers and shakers as well.

TWELVE

Survival Strategies for Caring Parents

Technology and increased knowledge may appear to make raising children in the "new millennium" an easier task than it was a century or decade ago. The truth is, however, that caring parents still need a strategy to help their children succeed. The old adage goes, "Those who plan for nothing get exactly what they planned for."

It is true that Americans enjoy unprecedented privileges, freedoms and options when making life choices for themselves and their families. However, many of those freedoms—such as the right to decide how our children are educated and how to raise them—are being whittled down and removed at an astounding pace.

While many federal programs and directives provide special services for children diagnosed with physical disabilities or labeled with learning disabilities such as ADHD, ADD or autistic spectrum disorders, parents often must fight for their children's best interests. This happens most often in the areas of health and medical decisions, educational services and social standing (denying others the right to wrongly *label* a child with the stigma of "ADHD or ADD").

If you will establish an organized strategy for your child

in advance, you may be able to avoid many of the especially difficult problems others have encountered over the years. This applies regardless of your child's social, physical and psychological characteristics.

Caring parents have the right to *impose* their values and expectations for their children on everyone who has access to them. Much as the members of a large family might "firmly" and pointedly introduce themselves—including a long line of muscular male relatives...father, brothers, uncles and grandfather—to a young man wanting to take a pretty female member of the family on a date, there is a legitimate point to be made to medical professionals, school teachers and administrators, government represen-tatives and friends. That unspoken or spoken point is this:

> This is *my child*—he is not a number, he is not a statis-tic, he is not a "subject on a chart," and above all, he is *not* an experimental test subject for pet theories, unproven procedures or unsafe substances of any kind. I will hold you personally responsible for the decisions you make, the actions you take and the methods you use with him. We are looking forward to a *good* and *safe* experience shared in full cooperation. I am not aban-doning my child to your control; I am entrusting him temporarily in your care while retaining full legal, spir-itual and familial physical rights over my child as his parent, protector and legal guardian. This means I also retain the right to examine your performance and dis-agree with your opinions or procedures at any point in time and seek second opinions or to remove my child from your influence or temporary control.

While I do not recommend an antagonistic attitude toward organizations, institutions and the individuals who work for them, I *do* strongly recommend that you *impose* your loving *care* and diligent *concern* for your child's well-being.

WINNING THAT "EXTRA MEASURE OF CARE"

An athletic coach tends to deal more carefully with children whose parents are "in the stands" during sports practice sessions or events. Similarly, medical professionals, teachers and other workers tend to add an extra measure of care and diligence when they know Mom or Dad are carefully and thoughtfully examining everything they say and do while working with a child.

In my experience, it sometimes takes pointed communication to jar certain people in institutional settings who are deeply entangled in a rigid "institutional mind-set." It is vital to take a determined *personal interest* in your child's education, healthcare and development from birth to full adulthood. The welfare of your child is at stake. The government is not called or equipped to raise and nurture your child—*you are*.

Ideally, you should begin your strategy even before your children are conceived. Many parents-to-be wisely change their diets, personal habits and lifestyles to help their children who will come along later. It is a fact that unhealthy mothers will probably produce unhealthy babies. Parents who drink excessive amounts of alcohol, take recreational drugs or take dangerous prescription drugs at the time a child is conceived may well damage the DNA chromosomes of their unborn child!

STRATEGIC TIPS FOR THE PRECONCEPTION PHASE

If you haven't started your family yet, or if you anticipate having another child in the near future, we suggest you follow a preconception diet. A preconception diet is similar to a prenatal diet with the main difference being fasting.

Before conception, we suggest that both partners fast one day a week to cleanse their bodies of toxic waste, to heal tissues and organs and to help strengthen their bodies. Reasonable fasting also helps the body return to its ideal body weight, which is especially helpful for moms-to-be.[1] (Warning: If you have a history of blood-sugar problems, do *not* go on a fast except with the approval and guidance of your physician. Women who have already conceived should not fast while carrying a baby either.)

If you are a mom-to-be, you need to retrain your mind and start thinking—and eating—for two. You should be eating fresh grains, seeds and nuts, fresh vegetables and fruits, plus a little bit of fish, chicken and maybe a little bit of turkey.

Grains, seeds and nuts are excellent sources of protein, vitamin E and the B vitamins, plus they are nature's best source of unsaturated fatty acids such as lecithin. Seeds in particular are very high in enzyme and trace minerals that you normally can't get in your diet through other means. Seeds also contain high levels of manganese, a very important nutrient for the reproductive system.

Eggs are excellent food sources for preconception, but only if they are "yard eggs," which come from chickens that lay eggs in the natural way without injected hormones, steroids or antibiotics. Basically, healthy chickens lay good eggs. The yolks are more yellow, and the eggs contain lots of lecithin. The shell of a yard egg is actually harder because there's more calcium in it.

As much as possible, avoid any foods that might be laced with contaminants such as hormones, steroids, antibiotics or environmental chemicals such as herbicides and insecticides. Whenever possible, purchase "organic" or "organically grown" grains, chicken, beef and so forth. Cow's milk from the grocery story probably contains some of these contaminants in trace amounts. Goat's milk, while unconventional in the minds of most people, is actually better for you and is most likely free of such contaminants.

Begin a regular course of exercise at least three times a week. Avoid food and beverage products containing caffeine and alcohol. Cut back or eliminate sugar from your diet (in all forms). Get plenty of sleep, and drink at least eight glasses of purified water a day (distilled or purified by reverse osmosis). Make sure you eat enough protein as part of a balanced diet each day, and be sure you take enough folic acid (this helps prevent certain birth defects). Supplement your diet with natural vitamins each day.

STRATEGIC TIPS
FOR THE PRENATAL PHASE

If you learn that you are a new mother-to-be (if you are a new father-to-be, share this with your partner), immediately modify your diet and lifestyle to follow all of the tips we just covered for preconception (with the exception of fasting, which is a no-no for pregnant women).

Give your unborn child every possible advantage you can. Again, eat the right foods, avoid harmful foods (and environmental contaminants), exercise regularly and appropriately, drink plenty of purified water and pray over your child often. Here are some nutritional tips (make sure you consult closely with your family doctor, obstetrician/gynecologist, pediatrician or healthcare provider) to make sure you are providing the necessary nutrients for both yourself and for your unborn child.

Many people believe all of their nutritional needs are met simply by eating a balanced diet, but times have changed. This *might* be true:

❑ If you live on a farm free of all pesticides and herbicides.

❑ If everything you eat is fresh and you drink clean water free of all pollution and contamination.

❑ If you eat four to six different vegetables a day and three to six different kinds of fruit.

❑ If you get all the protein you need from uncontaminated low-fat sources.

In this case, *perhaps* you don't need any supplements (assuming the soil hasn't been depleted of all its nutrients or contaminated with pesticides laid down thirty years ago). But who today can do that?

The logical solution is to supplement your diet with natural vitamins. (Most of the vitamins available through mass retailers and discount chains are less expensive than those sold in the better health food stores for a good reason—they aren't harvested from nature. They are "manufactured synthetically" in chemical plants. If that doesn't sound very healthy to you, then you're grasping the situation.)

Avoid all synthetic chemical vitamins because many of them are made from coal tar derivatives (they are *petroleum*-based), and they don't feed tissue cells. You need a natural supplement that will provide vital nutrients to your body cells. (Call my office at 800-726-1834 if you want help selecting and purchasing high-quality vitamins and supplements for maximum health.)

A CHEAP PRICE GUARANTEES CHEAP NUTRITION

I'm well aware that vitamins and food supplements can be expensive, but avoid the temptation to go for the cheapest products you can find at drug store specials and on large discount chain bargain tables. You will get exactly what you pay for: A cheap price only guarantees that you get cheap nutrition. Of all the investments you make each day, this should be one area where you invest in the best for your own health and the health of your loved ones.

A good multivitamin isn't enough by itself, but it is an

excellent start. Choose a good multivitamin that contains at least one-third of the government's RDA for pregnant women at the very least. Make sure it contains no sugar or fillers and that it is made from a natural food source.

Include a natural B-complex vitamin supplement in your daily diet. B complex is a water-soluble vitamin, meaning that it is depleted on a daily basis. The B vitamins provide all kinds of benefits, but they effectively help us manage stress and strengthen the immune system.

Make sure your B vitamin includes 100 percent of the RDA for *biotin*. Biotin is a very expensive product, but you need about 500 milligrams a day for the development of your child.

There has been some evidence that morning sickness may be caused, in part, by a shortage of *folic acid*, which is generally found in good B-complex vitamins. Make sure your B-complex vitamin contains folic acid, which is also vital to the proper development of your unborn child's nervous system and brain.

You need a lot of *calcium* when you are pregnant. You need about 600 milligrams of calcium daily, along with 250 milligrams of *magnesium*, and 400 International Units of *vitamin D*. The best natural source of these vitamins may well be raw goat's milk. There's a big difference between raw and pasteurized goat's milk. The pasteurization process kills the enzyme that helps the body to absorb the calcium. If you prefer to use a vitamin supplement, then choose a natural calcium supplement that includes manganese and vitamin D, because those components help your body absorb the calcium.

AFTER YOUR CHILD IS BORN

Carefully study the information provided in this book concerning childhood immunizations, and conduct your own research. Talk *in advance* with your healthcare provider about any concerns you may have.[2]

Since much of your child's learning takes place in the first seven years of life, *you* have an unequaled opportunity to help your child get a "jump on life." Provide your child with proper attitudes, moral values, godly character traits and an early love of learning that will serve him or her well throughout life!

Consciously create a strategy for success for your child. He is naturally curious about his world, the people around him and what makes things work. Fill his "universe" with fascinating opportunities to learn, discover, experiment and question. Don't wait until he is four years old to introduce him to your local library. Take him with you when he is two, and let him pick out colorful books that attract his eye.

Don't merely focus on moving from point A to point B. Constantly examine your surroundings for opportunities to teach your child about the wonders of God's universe. Don't just point at a tree and say the word. Let her feel the bark, tap the root or base with her toe, hug the tree trunk to get a sense of its circumference and trace the delicate patterns on its leaves.

INVEST THE TIME TO SMELL THE ROSES

Make sure your child picks an orange from an orange tree, helps pick a watermelon from a field, harvests potatoes from the soil or plucks a ripe apple from the tree (depending on your geographic location). Invest the time to smell the roses, plunge those young fingers in the cool soil of the garden, throw rocks in the pond, pet the dog and feel the breeze of a cool December wind.

One of the most important things you can do for your children is to teach them how to eat healthy foods early. As I noted in my book *Maximum Energy*, the U.S. Department of Agriculture (USDA) issued a report written by Dr. Mark Hecksted of the Harvard School of Public Health that said:

I wish to stress that there is a great deal of evidence that continues to accumulate, which strongly implicates, and in some instances proves, that the major causes of death and disability in the United States are related to the diet that we eat. I include coronary artery disease, heart disease (which accounts for nearly half of the deaths in the United States), several of the most important forms of cancer, hypertension, diabetes and obesity, as well as other chronic diseases.[3]

Let me warn you that your chances of success in any effort to teach your child proper dietary choices decrease with each hour he spends in front of the television *if you do not have a strategy or plan.* I know this may sound extreme, but you should never underestimate the persuasive power of television *or* of the child who sits in front of it.

For every parental encouragement and requirement you make about healthy food choices, the "idiot-box" will flood your child's mind and senses with *hundreds of thirty-second promotions.* Your child will be targeted by ads hyping sugary breakfast cereals, allergy-inducing dairy products, fast-food restaurant entrees (offering high-fat, high-cholesterol, low-nutrition foods that seem positively habit-forming), prepackaged frozen delights filled with chemical additives, preservatives, colorings, flavorings and very little true nutrition value.

YOU NEED A STRATEGY!

Television is here to stay, and so are those commercials and the "food" products and poor choices they promote. That means the buck stops with you. Believe me, you will need a *strategy* just to hold the line for yourself!

If you doubt the power of television, ask your friends or the parents of young children in your church or neighborhood at what age their children could point out the logos and even name or sing the advertisement jingle of particular fast-food restaurants. Many parents say their children could do one or all of these things *before* they could even string together a sentence!

Don't go into the battle without a ready-made strategy. Make the plan, then work the plan. It is difficult, but you and your child will reap a lifetime of better health if you follow through faithfully, consistently and persistently.

We have already offered some dietary suggestions for newborn infants and toddlers in this book. *Train Up Your Children in the Way They Should Eat*, written by my wife, Sharon, offers more dietary guidelines. (Call my office at 800-726-1834 to obtain your personal copy.) Remember also that this is the period in your child's life when an adequate supply of vitamin A is absolutely essential to the proper development of his brain, nervous system, autoimmune system and his digestive system (the gut).

PRESCHOOL AND ELEMENTARY SCHOOL PHASE

The years leading up to your child's first school experience present a number of crucial decisions for caring parents. In most cases, school systems require that your child be immunized or present a legal waiver for non-immunization before your child can enter the educational system. It is in preschool, kindergarten and first grade that your child receives his first exposure to whatever reading system the school system uses.

My personal recommendation is that you invest some money in a good phonics early reader program (available through my office) and personally teach your child to read *before* he ever enters a formal classroom. Children can easily learn to read and *enjoy it* at the age of two or three. The only requirement is that they be able to talk. This simple strategy can open a door of learning that will only grow with every year of life.

If your child does well at home but seems to have problems in a classroom setting, that should be a "red flag" warning you that more investigation is needed. Personally sit in on classes to see how the teacher interacts with your child and the others in the room, and examine the teaching curriculum to see of some "modern" variation of whole-word techniques are being used. Make sure your child isn't eating "problem" foods at school that fuel hyperactivity or cause attention problems.

By this time, you should have completed your research and made your decision about immunizations. If you decided not to have your child immunized, then make sure you know the particular vaccination laws or regulations in your state and region. Many states permit "waivers" of vaccination requirements based on philosophical objections or general religious belief.

TIMELY INTERVENTION

It is during the first few years of organized education that we see the highest percentage of children diagnosed or labeled with ADHD, ADD or autistic spectrum disorders. Early intervention with vitamin A (1 to 2 tablespoons of cod liver oil daily), revised or elimination diets devoid of suspect foods, and well-informed decisions concerning immunizations may help prevent or eliminate these problems in your child's life.

You may need the council and expertise of a competent physician while wading through evidence for and against childhood immunizations. Make sure you choose a doctor who is well informed in the area of proper nutrition and the latest research available for ADHD, ADD and autistic spectrum disorders. If at all possible, find a doctor who maintains at least a neutral or objective stance on compulsory immunizations and drug therapy for children with ADHD and ADD. Find a physician who is more interested in treating the *cause* of a problem than in writing a quick prescription to treat its symptoms.

A few states make it very difficult for parents to exempt their children from vaccinations. In those cases, you can still consider the homeschooling alternative (an alternative my wife and I heartily recommend), membership in a legal church organization that specifically includes the avoidance of vaccinations as part of their religious tenets or moving to a more reasonable state.

As difficult as these interventions may seem (particularly the elimination diets), they are far easier and less dangerous than placing your child on a lifetime prescription of such powerful and potentially addictive medications as Ritalin or any its cousins. These include Concerta, Cylert, Prozac, Dexedrine, Adderall, Tofranil, Paxil, Luvox, Risperdal, Depakote, clonidine, Tenex, Neurontin or even lithium.

All of these medications have potentially dangerous side effects, and the *long-term* effects for many of these medications are unknown (especially where the bodies of school-age and adolescent children are concerned).

That an over-the-counter substance so seemingly harmless as aspirin would be linked to Reyes syndrome was unthinkable just a few years ago. The drugs used to "treat" ADHD and ADD are far more powerful than aspirin.

WHAT DO YOU HAVE TO LOSE?

You should *really* try to deal with any behavioral or learning problems using the nutritional and educational interventions offered in this book before committing to such a radical course of medical intervention. What do you and your child have to lose?

If you decide to have your child immunized, then always ask for mercury-free preparations. Demand the DTaP vaccine rather than the DTP, and make sure your child receives consistent doses of vitamin A *before* and *after* any and all injections. Ask to spread out the vaccinations as well since some researchers feel accelerated injections may produce accelerated problems in children.

If your child has developed symptoms of ADHD, ADD or autistic spectrum disorders, immediately remove excess sugar, food dyes and key problem foods from her diet if necessary. Also begin vitamin A therapy immediately, and arm yourself with information about the special services available for your child.

Many parents of children with learning disabilities, and particularly those with autistic spectrum disorders, face an uphill battle in their fight to get appropriate and competent assistance for their children—but the battle is winnable. At least in this area, you have federal law on your side.

Seek out parents of other autistic spectrum children, contact one or more of the national autism organizations and arm yourself for the battle. I recommend that you be courteous, but never give up the fight.

Your child's well-being is at stake, and he will never have a more passionate advocate than *you*. Remember, all it takes for a revolution is one person with courage. You may need the same courage when dealing with your health provider as well. Nearly all doctors and nurse practitioners are sincere and mean well, but that doesn't mean they have what it takes to "buck the status quo" and seek out the best course of treatment for your child—especially if it goes in the face of politically correct medical practice.

Don't be afraid to hold accountable your child's doctors, teachers, school counselors, special education workers, school administrators and the local school board. Any and all of these are capable of siphoning away your right as a parent to make all the important decisions concerning your child's education, medical care and proper treatment.

PREPARED FOR LIFE

Be proactive and do everything in your power to prepare your children for success in life. Teach them how to read *yourself* using phonics, and do it early so they won't turn out like so many of my college students years ago. Many of those young people were functionally illiterate because they had been pushed through the educational system and promoted "on the curve" rather than held accountable for poor academic performance.

In some cases, when I included true/false questions on my exams, some of these students actually left the true/false questions blank! Even if you don't know anything about a particular subject, you have a 50/50 probability of *guessing* the right answer, so you should never just leave them blank.

The situation quickly deteriorated even further when I asked a short essay question. Many of my university students simply couldn't articulate themselves on paper. I knew my days in the university system were short when one of the professors told me, "It's really important not to fail anybody." When I asked him what he meant, he said, "Well, you know we have certain government quotas that we have to meet. If the students fail, we lose the government subsidies."

You can avoid the mediocrity syndrome by starting your child on the road of literacy *early* with a solid foundation in phonics combined with a love for learning. As a parent, you, more than any other, have your child's best interests at heart. One of the best gifts you can give your child is a solid preparation for success in life. It takes preplanning and effort, but it is worth it.

The important of advance preparation was driven home to me in 1977 when I went camping with a friend in the Great Smoky Mountains. During the month of April, weather conditions could change very suddenly and very drastically.

An unexpected snowstorm descended on the mountain range, and my friend and I were caught right in the middle of it on the top of the mountain. We abandoned our plan to spend the night in a three-sided shelter because the wind-chill factor had dropped to 20 degrees below zero. We had sleeping bags, but we brought only one ground pad with us. Whoever drew the short straw would have to sleep without a ground pad and face a risk of freezing to death.

We knew there were some cottages and a small lodge higher up, so we hiked up there through the falling snow. The cottages were closed for the season, but we found an attendant and asked if we could please spend the night in one of the empty cottages. There still wasn't any heat, but at least we could close the door, stay out of the wind and keep warm enough in our sleeping bags.

The real lesson in the value of preparation came the next day. The storm had passed, leaving behind bright blue skies and the incredible beauty of the wild mountainous terrain. Yet, even though the rough weather has passed, the pine trees around us were still covered with snow, and we faced a very real danger of ice coating the trail off the mountain.

WE COULD HELP BECAUSE
WE WERE PREPARED

We had to cross a pair of extremely steep and ice-coated cliffs, but we had no problem since we had brought ice crampons and ropes with us. We ran into some other hikers who had actually been stranded by an equally dangerous ice coating, but we were able to help them cross the dangerous passage by stretching a guide rope between my friend and me. In other words, we actually were able to help those people get off the mountain *because we were prepared*.

The moral of the story is that I didn't prepare to spend night in 20-below-zero temperatures because I knew I could probably spend the night in a lodge if I had to. However, I did pack ice crampons and climbing ropes just in case we had to cross treacherous ice patches on the mountain's steep trails.

Just as preparation helped to save our hiking trip, so preparation can insure your children's future success. Begin by teaching them how to eat the right kind of foods for maximum health and energy. Teach and model godly character traits using the appropriate types of discipline with even consistency. If you want your child to be prepared for life, then teach him the skills of an entrepreneur or show her how to land a good job and keep it by being a good employee.

No matter who you are or what circumstances you face in life, you can help your children achieve their maximum potential in life if you prepare them for success. The need for preplanning and consistent execution is even more important if your child faces the added challenges of ADHD, ADD or autistic spectrum disorder symptoms.

TEACH THEM TO KEEP THEIR WORD

One of the rarest qualities in America's schools (and therefore in its family settings), unfortunately, is honesty. I can still feel the sick feeling of deep disappointment I felt the day I caught my college technical assistant (or teaching assistant) cheating on an exam.

This young man was a good student and a former member of the military services. He was also a student in one of my classes. When I ordered photocopies of the final exam for this class, for some reason the administrative office called upon this student assistant to pick up the copies and bring to me. I'd ordered forty copies of the exam for my thirty-five students (it is common practice to order extras copies in case any of the copies were unreadable or had omitted pages).

When I pulled the package from my in-box, I found only thirty-eight copies. I assumed it was just a minor mistake until I noticed that this assistant and one other young man had managed to complete the hourlong exam in only twelve minutes.

My suspicions were confirmed when both young men made 100 percent on the tests (the average score in the class was 82 percent, and every other student used the full hour to complete the exam). The administration initially encouraged me to confront the young men about the evidence, and they quickly denied wrongdoing. At that point the administration absolved itself from the situation, and I was forced to drop the complaint.

DISHONESTY AFFECTS FAMILIES, BUSINESSES AND NATIONS

Personal dishonesty has a way of affecting family members, businesses and even national reputations in some cases. My wife and I visited the nation of Turkey with some friends several years ago to conduct extensive research into the Turkish diet. My friend wanted a Turkish rug, and we each decided to purchase small 4- x 6-foot rugs. They were hand-loomed masterpieces that took nearly eighteen months to make.

My original plan was to roll up the rug and haul it back to Florida in my suitcase, but the Turkish merchant said, "Oh no, no. I'll ship it. That way you don't have to deal with the hassle of declaring it through customs. Plus, you won't have to carry it for the next two weeks on the cruise and while you're traveling in Europe." Then he said, "I'll ship it straight to your house, and by the time you get home, the rug will be there waiting for you."

You probably know the rest of the story at this point. Since my friend was in favor of shipping both rugs, I agreed to leave the rug with the seller so he could ship it directly to my home—but the rug never came.

Fortunately, I was smart enough to pay for the purchase with a major credit card in case I had to put a "back charge" on it if something fell through. Sure enough, when we arrived home in the States, the rug wasn't there. Finally, after waiting for four weeks, I called Turkey and discovered the seller would not answer the phone. When the credit card company back-charged the purchase amount, the man in Turkey claimed that he'd shipped the rug, but he couldn't produce a receipt with my signature—because he'd never sent it.

We received a refund six months later, and we also received phone calls from members of the man's family in Turkey who offered again to sell us the rug (we politely declined their offer). They said members of the family were chasing their unscrupulous relative around the area because he had disgraced them with his dishonesty in a number of situations. During this chase his car ran off a cliff and he was killed. As the old adage goes, "Honesty is the best policy" (and it is the building block for success in the lives of our children).

YOU ARE NOT HELPLESS, AND YOU ARE NOT ALONE

If you purchased this book because your child has *already* been labeled with the ADHD, ADD or autistic-spectrum stigma, I pray that it has encouraged and empowered you. I wrote this book to help you understand that you are not helpless and powerless in this situation—when it is all said and done, *you* are the one who tucks in your child each night and provides his or her needs day after day, week after week and year after year. *And you are not alone.* Millions of caring parents like you are also struggling with the same issues and problems.

There is much you can do for your child and for yourself. At the risk of being redundant, I encourage you to arm yourself with knowledge, link arms with other caring parents and professionals from the medical and educational communities, and step to the front of the crowd and let your caring voices be heard.

Make your case for responsible and careful medical research and public health policy. Persistently demand proven and effective teaching methodologies in the public schools. If the officials don't listen, then make a plan with your allies and get yourself *elected to the school board.* When it comes to caring for your child and protecting his future, no one on this planet can do it as well as you can.

Finally, I encourage you to pray. Pray over every aspect of your family situation. Seek divine guidance in everything. On those especially dark days when no one seems to be listening and you fear you've lost the will to fight, take courage in knowing God is listening and that prayer changes things. Please, if you have any questions, call me at (800) 726-1834.

NOTES

Introduction
Reaping a Bitter Harvest

1. National Institute of Mental Health (NIMH) prediction cited by Jan Eastgate, "Propaganda by Redefinition of Words—the Betrayal of Our Children," *Psychiatry: Betraying & Drugging Children* (Los Angeles: Citizens Commission on Human Rights International, 1998), 2.

2. J. M. Zito, D. J. Safer, S. dosReis, J. F. Gardner, J. Boles and F. Lynch, "Trends in the prescribing of psychotropic medications to preschoolers," *Journal of American Medical Disabilities* (2000).

3. Cited by Peter R. Breggin, M.D., in sworn testimony before the Subcommittee on Oversight and Investigations, Committee on Education and the Workforce, U.S. House of Representatives, September 29, 2000. Dr. Breggin is a psychiatrist and the founder and director of the International Center for the Study of Psychiatry and Psychology. Accessed via the Internet at www.breggin.com/congress.html on 6/28/01.

4. Ibid.

5. Lawrence H. Diller, M.D., "Kids on Drugs," an Internet article appearing in the Health & Body page of salon.com at www.salon.com/health/feature/2000/03/09/kid_drugs. Dr. Lawrence H. Diller practices behavioral pediatrics in Walnut Creek, CA. He is the author of *Running on Ritalin: A Physician Reflects on Children, Society, and Performance in a Pill* (New York: Bantam Books, 1999).

6. Breggin, cited above.

7. Ted Broer, "The Dangers of Prescribed Psychiatric Medications," an article prepared by the author for distribution to patients and subscribers, page 17, citing Lewis A. Opler, M.D., Ph.D., and Carol Bialkowski, *Prozac and Other Psychiatric Drugs* (New York: Pocket Books, a div. of Simon and Schuster, 1996), 26–29.

Chapter 1
Filtering the Hype From "Attention-Deficit Hyperactivity Disorder"

1. Robert S. Mendelsohn, M.D., *Confessions of a Medical Heretic* (Chicago, IL: Contemporary Books, an imprint of NTC/Contemporary Publishing Company, 1979), 33. Dr. Mendelsohn wrote the nationally syndicated column and subscription newsletter, "The People's Doctor," and was the national medical director of Project Head Start and chairman of the Medical Licensure Committee for the state of Illinois. He was associate professor of Preventive Medicine and Community Health in the School of Medicine of the University of Illinois and director of Michael Reese Hospital in Chicago, Illinois. He was a leading critic of modern medical practices whose books, articles and professional accomplishments helped stimulate significant improvements in the way medicine is practiced in the United States. His other books include *Male [mal]practice: How Doctors Manipulate Women* (Chicago: Contemporary Books, 1981) and *How to Raise a Healthy Child...in Spite of Your Doctor* (New York: Ballantine Books, a div. of Random House, 1987).

2. Dr. Mary Ann Block, *No More Ritalin: Treating ADHD Without Drugs: A Mother's Journey, A Physician's Approach* (New York: Kensington Books, 1996), 18; Robert S. Mendelsohn, M.D., *How to Raise a Healthy Child...in Spite of Your Doctor* (New York: Ballantine Books, 1987), 220.

3. Fred A. Baughman, Jr., M.D., "Educational 'Disorders' Fraud," an article appearing in *Psychiatry: Betraying & Drugging Children*, 10–11.

4. Cited in Kelley Patricia O'Meara, "Doping Kids," *Insight Magazine* (June 28, 1999): 13.

5. American Psychiatric Association, *Diagnostic and Statistical Manual of Mental Disorders, Fourth Edition* (DSM-IV).

6. Diller, "Kids on Drugs."

7. O'Meara, "Doping Kids," 12.

8. Ibid.

9. Rod Stafford, "Ritalin and Cocaine: A Pattern of Abuse," *NBC Dateline Special Report,* January 16, 2001, from television interview with Gretchen Poisner, DEA pharmacologist.

10. It is obvious that most single parents didn't ask for the difficult task of raising their children single-handedly, but even the most conscientious parent occasionally forgets that the added burden imposed by the absence of a parent (although necessary or even beneficial in some instances involving abuse) places stress on the children as well as on the remaining parent.

Chapter 2
What to Do First: Educate Yourself

1. Mendelsohn, *How to Raise a Healthy Child...in Spite of Your Doctor,* 12.

2. Ibid., 21.

3. Ibid., 9.

4. Ibid., 9–10. Dr. Mendelsohn discussed this point in greater detail on page 20: "The pediatrician's wanton prescribing of powerful drugs indoctrinates children from birth with the philosophy of 'a pill for every ill.' This may lead the child to the belief that there is a drug to treat every condition and that drugs are an appropriate response to normal feelings of frustration, depression, anxiety, inadequacy, insecurity, etc. Doctors are directly responsible for hooking millions of people on prescription drugs. They are also indirectly responsible for the plight of millions more who turn to illegal drugs because they were taught at an early age that drugs can cure anything—including psychological and emotional conditions—that ails them."

5. Mendelsohn, *Confessions of a Medical Heretic,* 33. Dr. Mendelsohn published this book in 1979 when the ADD/ADHD ball was just beginning to roll. His numbers are seriously outdated, but his point still stands.

6. Block, *No More Ritalin.*

7. Ibid., 5.

8. I do not mean to favor osteopathic physicians over other kinds of healthcare providers in this book. This was the case in Mary Ann Block's life. Some osteopathic physicians practice medicine with a narrow predisposition toward drug therapy and surgery, while certain medical doctors approach medical care with a truly holistic and "osteo-pathic" view, avoiding drugs and surgery except as a last option. You may choose to seek a health provider from the totally different health disciplines. The key is to educate yourself so you can make informed decisions about health-care for yourself and your loved ones.

9. Block, *No More Ritalin*, 10.

10. Ibid., p. 12.

11. The *Physicians' Desk Reference (PDR)* is a valuable source of information, but it should never be used to self-diag-nose physical problems or arbitrarily change medication dosages. Consult your health professional before chang-ing or ending a drug therapy.

12. Mendelsohn, *How to Raise a Healthy Child...in Spite of Your Doctor*, 8.

13. The most visible national support organization in the United States is called Children and Adults with Attention Deficit Disorder (CHADD), but you should be aware that it is largely supported by donations from drug manufacturers.

Chapter 3
Ritalin—Educating the Medicated:
Why Do We Drug Our Kids?

1. Developed from figures cited by psychiatrist Peter R. Breggin, M.D., in sworn testimony before the Subcommittee on Oversight and Investigations, Committee on Education and the Workforce, U.S. House of Representatives, September 29, 2000. Accessed via the Internet at www.breggin.com/congress.html on 6/28/01.

2. Karen Thomas, "Ritalin Maker's Ties to Advocates Probed," *USA Today* (November 16, 1995): accessed via Internet 1/04/00 at http://usatoday.elibrary.com/s/usatoday.

3. Ibid.

4. Susan Brink, "Doing Ritalin right: Sure, it works—but there are big flaws in the way it's being given," *U.S. News & World Report* (November 23, 1998): 76–81, emphasis mine.

5. Breggin, congressional testimony cited above.

6. "Federal Judge Dismisses ADHD Lawsuit," News Release No. 01-17, March 13, 2001, American Psychiatric Association, accessed via the Internet at http://psych.org.

7. Breggin, congressional testimony cited above.

8. Karen Thomas, "Study of attention deficit disorder supports medicine over therapy" *USA Today* (December 15, 1999): 14D. Accessed via Internet 1/04/00 at http://usatoday.elibrary.com/s/usatoday. Note: This NIMH study was not subjected to scientific review by peers at the time, and it claimed to demonstrate that Ritalin appeared to more effectively relieve "core symptoms" of attention and concentration problems, overactivity, impulsivity and distractibility while not doing as well with "non-ADHD symptoms" such as social skills, relationships and reading. It was published in the *Archives of General Psychiatry* (emphasis mine).

9. Breggin, congressional testimony cited above.

10. Anita Manning, "'90s Teens Abusing Ritalin," *USA Today* (March 14, 1995): accessed via the Internet at http://usatoday.elibrary.com/s/usatoday.

11. Karen Thomas, "Cause of Attention Deficit?" *USA Today* (November 9, 1995): accessed via the Internet 1/04/00 at http://usatoday.elibrary.com/s/usatoday.

12. Karen Thomas, "Study May Shed Light on ADD," *USA Today* (November 24, 1998): accessed via the Internet 1/04/00 at http://usatoday.elibrary.com/s/usatoday.

13. Ibid., emphasis mine.

14. Breggin, congressional testimony cited above.

15. Ibid.

16. Doreen Iudica Vigue, "Ritalin use challenged," *The Boston Globe* (January 21, 2000): accessed via the Internet

at www.boston.com/dailyglobe2/021/metro/Ritalin_use_
challenged+.shtml.

17. "Psychiatry Stigmatizes and Harms Children," *Psychiatry:
A Human Rights Abuse and Global Failure* (Los Angeles:
Citizens Commission on Human Rights International,
2000), accessed via the Internet at
www.cchr.org/failure/eng/page33.htm on 7-16-01.

18. Diller, "Kids on Drugs." He is the author of *Running on
Ritalin: A Physician Reflects on Children, Society, and
Performance in a Pill* (New York: Bantam Books, 1999).

19. Ibid. Dr. Diller has treated more than two thousand children "who struggle with behavior and performance at
home or at school." He became "increasingly uneasy"
with the role he played and the readiness of everyone
involved to medicate children after he obtained information from the National Disease and Therapeutic index of
IMS Health. (IMS Health, in Dr. Diller's words, "is to
drug companies what the A.C. Nielson Company is to
television networks." He explained that the pharmaceutical industry relies on it to report on the latest trends in
medication usage.) The drug usage figures he quotes in
this article come from this index.

20. Ibid.

21. William G. Crook, M.D, Letter to the Editor, "Ritalin
controls symptoms, but causes remain," *USA Today*
(April 14, 1998): 14A. Accessed via the Internet at
http://usatoday.elibrary.com/s/usatoday.

22. Diller, "Kids on Drugs."

23. Ibid.

24. Ibid.

25. Ibid.

26. Ibid., emphasis mine.

27. Marilyn Elias, "Kids and depression: Are drugs the
answer?" *USA Today* (November 30, 1999): accessed via
the Internet at http://usatoday.elibrary.com/s/usatoday.
The central focus of this article was upon the estimated
half million children in the U.S. taking prescribed SSRI
antidepressants such as Prozac, Zoloft and Paxil, but the

author also dealt with widespread off-label prescription of psychiatric medications to children.

28. Diller, "Kids on Drugs."

29. Ibid.

30. Ibid.

31. Breggin, congressional testimony cited above.

Chapter 4
Do Treatments Pass or Fail?

1. Cited in "Psychiatry: A History of Failure," *Documenting Psychiatry—a Human Rights Abuse and Global Failure* (Los Angeles: Citizens Commission on Human Rights International, 2000–2001).

2. "Getting Hooked: The Sacred Cow of Psychiatric Rituals—Child Drug Pushing," *Harming Lives: Psychiatry Betraying & Drugging Children* (Los Angeles: Citizens Commission on Human Rights International, 1998), 13.

3. "Psychiatry: A History of Failure," *Documenting Psychiatry.*

4. Elliot S. Valenstein, Ph.D., *Blaming the Brain* (New York: The Free Press, 1998), 150.

5. Edward Shorter, *A History of Psychiatry: From the Era of the Asylums to the Age of Prozac* (New York: John Wiley & Sons, Inc., 1997), 289.

6. Brink, "Doing Ritalin right: Sure, it works—but there are big flaws in the way it's being given."

7. "Psychiatry: A History of Failure," *Documenting Psychiatry.*

8. Valenstein, *Blaming the Brain,* 162.

9. John Leo, "Doing the Disorder Rag," On Society Column, *U.S. News & World Report* (October 27, 1997): accessed via the Internet at www.usnews.com/usnews/issue/971027/27john.htm.

10. "Psychiatry: A History of Failure," *Documenting Psychiatry.*

11. The Discovery Channel, citing a Reuters report citing a study described in *Perspectives in Biology and Medicine* (Summer 2001). Accessed through the Discovery Channel Internet site at http://dsc.discovery.com/news/reu/20010716/lincoln.html.

12. "Getting Hooked: The Sacred Cow of Psychiatric Rituals—Child Drug Pushing," 8–11.

13. Franz G. Alexander, M.D. and Sheldon T. Selesnick, M.D., *The History of Psychiatry* (NY: Harper & Row, 1966), 163.

14. Valenstein, *Blaming the Brain*, 205.

15. Peter Shrag, *Mind Control* (Pantheon Books, 1978), 42.

16. Henry A. Foley and Steven S. Sharfstein, *Madness and Government* (Washington, DC: American Psychiatric Press, Inc., 1983), 29.

17. Thomas Szasz, M.D., *Cruel Compassion* (New York: John Wiley & Sons, Inc., 1994), 166.

18. Diller, "Kids on Drugs."

19. Ibid.

20. Matthew Daly, Associated Press (July 17, 2001): accessed via the Internet at www.washingtonpost.com/wp-srv/aponline/20010717/aponline163217_000.ht.

21. Diller, "Kids on Drugs."

22. Daly, Associated Press (July 17, 2001).

23. Ibid.

24. Ibid.

25. Thomas Moore, *Prescription for Disaster: The Hidden Dangers in Your Medicine Cabinet* (New York: Simon & Schuster, 1998).

26. Ibid., 88, quoting Katzen-Ellenbogen's trial testimony, cited in "Politics of Psychiatry."

27. Michael Coren, "The Origin of Social Engineering," *The Financial Post* (18 September 1997); "Swedes resent scapegoat role in eugenics controversy," *Financial Times* (6 September 1997).

28. "Forgotten Shame, The Ethnic Cleansing of the 'Mentally Unfit' in Canada," *Freedom* (1997).

29. Ibid.; Tony Hall, "Eugenics scandal warrants inquiry, A fuller accounting from government medical profession," *The Edmonton Journal* (20 April 1998).

30. "Tvångssteriliserade kan fä ersättning," *Svenska Dagbladet* (26 January 1999).

31. Peter R. Breggin, M.D., in sworn testimony before the Subcommittee on Oversight and Investigations, Committee on Education and the Workforce, U.S. House of Representatives, September 29, 2000. Accessed via the Internet www.breggin.com/congress.html.

32. John Leo, "Numbers a Shrink Can Love," *U.S. News & World Report*, citing authors Herb Kutchins and Stuart Kirk, *Making Us Crazy—DSM: The Psychiatric Bible and the Creation of Mental Disorders* (New York: Free Press, 1997).

33. Leo, "Doing the Disorder Rag," emphasis mine.

34. Adapted from an article by Tim Friend, "Antidepressant use turns children into test subjects," *USA Today* (May 3, 1999): emphasis mine. Accessed via the Internet at http://usatoday.elibrary.com/s/usatoday.

35. O'Meara, "Doping Kids."

36. Ibid., 10–13. All information supplied in this bulleted list was adapted or quoted from this source.

37. Ibid., 11. The author also wrote with amazing clarity on page 13, "…there is *little evidence* to support a scientific basis for classifying ADHD as a mental illness. On the other hand, there is an *abundance of evidence* that stimulants such as Ritalin can produce symptoms such as mania, insomnia, hallucinations, hyperactivity, impulsivity and attacks of Tourette's or other tic syndromes"(emphasis mine).

38. "Psychiatry: A History of Failure," citing Valenstein, *Blaming the Brain*, 4, 6, 125, 224 (emphasis mine).

Chapter 5
The High/Low Jackpot:
Sugar Levels and Learning Levels

1. Crook, "Ritalin controls symptoms, but causes remain." Note: Dr. Crook is a fellow of the American Academy of Pediatrics, the American College of Allergists and the author of such books as *Solving the Puzzle of Your Hard-to-Raise Child* (New York: Random House, Inc., 1987)

and *Help for the Hyperactive Child: A practical guide offering parents of ADHD children alternatives to Ritalin* (Jackson, TN: Professional Books, 1991).

2. Janice Keller Phelps, M.D. and Alan E. Nourse, M.D., *The Hidden Addiction and How to Get Free* (New York: Little, Brown and Company, 1986), 73 (emphasis mine).

3. Crook, "Ritalin controls symptoms, but causes remain"(emphasis mine).

4. Ronald L. Hoffman, M.D., *The Natural Approach to Attention Deficit Disorder (ADD): Drug-free ways to treat the roots of this childhood epidemic* (New Canaan, CT: Keats Publishing, Inc., 1997), 15 (emphasis mine).

5. Ibid.

6. Ibid., 46–47, where Dr. Hoffman writes, "There is a phenomenon in medicine called the Inglefinger Effect that describes the way new medications and therapeutic procedures are introduced and become part of medical practice. When researchers introduce a new practice, there is usually tremendous initial skepticism and resistance; then gradually it is accepted, then wholeheartedly embraced. Finally, the pendulum can swing toward over enthusiasm and the practice becomes a therapeutic vogue…what ultimately emerges is a more balanced approach, where the excess of enthusiasm for the new practice is tempered; the practice becomes part of the medical arsenal, but does not eclipse all other approaches. When this happens, people are offered more individually tailored therapies instead of the therapy that's in vogue. This is what I think we will see in the case of ADD and ADHD: Ritalin will remain one of the treatment options, but [other] treatments and approaches…will become more common."

7. William G. Crook, M.D., *Help for the Hyperactive Child: A practical guide offering parents of ADHD children alternatives to Ritalin* (Jackson, TN: Professional Books, 1991), xvi.

8. Ibid.

9. Ted Broer, Ph.D., *Eat, Drink & Be Healthy Report*, Vol. 1, No. 1, 1995, citing L. Langseth and J. Dowd, "Glucose

tolerance and hyperkinesis," *FoodCosmetToxicol*, 16:129,1978.

10. Crook, *Help for the Hyperactive Child*, xvii.

11. Block, *No More Ritalin*, 73–74 (emphasis mine)

12. Ibid., 75.

Chapter 6
Your Child in a "Dumbed-Down" World

1. Jeanie Eller, noted reading and literacy expert, citing the United States Department of Education report, "A Nation at Risk," in an exclusive interview with the author in 2000.

2. The National Center for Family Literacy, "Research: Literacy Facts & Figures," citing figures from the National Adult Literacy Survey (NALS), 1993. Accessed 8/30/01 via the Internet at www.famlit.org/research/research.html#adult. The National Center for Family Literacy is a nonprofit educational organization based in Louisville, Kentucky, founded in 1989 with a grant from the William R. Kenan, Jr. Charitable Trust.

3. Scholastic Aptitude Test data for 1952–1994, Educational Testing Service, Princeton, New Jersey.

4. National Center for Education Statistics, "Findings From Education and the Economy: An Indicators Report," March 1997, under the subheading, "The literacy of a substantial portion of the U.S. labor force is limited, and only a small portion of workers perform at a high literacy level." Accessed via the Internet at http://nces.ed.gov/pubs97/97939.html.

5. Ibid.

6. Samuel L. Blumenfeld, *The Whole Language/OBE Fraud* (Boise, ID: The Paradigm Company, 1996), 295.

7. Ibid., 55, citing John Dewey, "The Primary-Education Fetich," *Forum*, Vol. XXV (May 1898): 315–328.

8. Ibid., 50–51.

9. Ms. Jeanie Eller has been featured on shows with Oprah

Winfrey, G. Gordon Liddy and Mary Matalin, as well as more than 3,000 other radio and television shows coast to coast. She taught school in Arizona for many years after earning her B.A. and M.A. at Arizona State University, and helped draft a new state law that will put phonics back into the Arizona schools. Eller also served on the Arizona State Education Board's committee for implementation of the law.

10. Samuel L. Blumenfeld, "Are Schools Causing the 'Attention Deficit Disorder' Epidemic?" *The Blumenfeld Education Letter* (September 1995): 3–4.

11. See Samuel L. Blumenfeld's *The New Illiterates* (Boise, ID: The Paradigm Co., 1973, 1988), for a detailed account of the dispute in 1844 between Horace Mann, then the Secretary of the Massachusetts Board of Education, who was "supported by the Harvard-Unitarian liberal establishment," and the conservative Boston schoolmasters.

12. Blumenfeld, *The Whole Language/OBE Fraud*, 34, citing an article written by John Edgar Johnson and published in "The Chinese Language," *The Biblioteca Sacra and Theological Eclectic* Vol. 30 (1873): 62–76.

13. Ibid., 41.

14. Ibid., 44.

15. Ibid., 66, citing G. Stanley Hall, *Educational Problems*, 2 vols. (New York: D. Appleton, 1911), 219.

16. Many years ago, Jeanie Eller discovered the Action Reading Program (developed by George Cureton) after the Anchorage, Alaska, School District asked her to find the best reading program in America. At this writing, Eller has been teaching the Action Reading Program for more than twenty-five years. The program includes a 100% money-back guarantee. You can order this program by calling my office at (800) 726-1834.

Chapter 7
Autism—the New Wave

1. Mary N. Megson, M.D., F.A.A.P., "Is Autism a G-Alpha

Protein Defect Reversible With Natural Vitamin A?",
citing testimony of R. Rollens before the United States
House Committee on Government Reform, August 3,
1999. Dr. Megson is a developmental pediatrician and an
assistant professor of pediatrics at the Medical College of
Virginia Hospital at Virginia Commonwealth University,
Pediatric and Adolescent Ability Center.

2. The Autism Society of America Foundation, "What Is
   Autism?", accessed 8/19/01 via the Internet at
   www.autism-society.org/whatisautism/autism.html.
   According to the ASA website, "The mission of the
   Autism Society of America is to promote lifelong access
   and opportunities for persons within the autism spectrum and their families to be fully included, participating
   members of their communities through advocacy, public
   awareness, education, and research related to autism." It
   was founded in 1965 by a small group of parents, and
   now has 24,000 members connected through a volunteer
   network of more than 240 chapters in 50 states.

3. Michael J. Goldberg, M.D., F.A.A.P., "A New Definition
   of Autism," accessed 9/3/99 via the Internet at www.neu-
   roimmunedr.com/Articles/Autism/New_Definition/body
   _new_definition.

4. Ibid.

5. 60 Minutes transcript, "Profile: The MMR vaccine; controversy surrounding British study that showed a link
   between autism and the vaccine for measles, mumps and
   rubella," 11/12/2000, CBS Television Network.

6. Rick Rollens, "Autism No. 1 Disability Entering
   California's Developmental Services System," FEAT
   Daily Newsletter, Sacramento, CA (August 19, 2001): the
   official online newsletter of the nonprofit Families for
   Early Autism Treatment, reporting on public news
   release by the California Department of Developmental
   Services office in Sacramento (emphasis mine). Accessed
   8-19-2001 via the Internet at www.feat.org/FEATnews.

7. Ibid.

8. From the testimony of Coleen Boyle, Ph.D., Chief,

Developmental Disabilities Branch, Division of Birth Defects, Child Development, and Disability and Health, National Center for Environmental Health, Centers For Disease Control and Prevention, Department of Health and Human Services, before the Government Reform Committee, U.S. House of Representatives, April 6, 2000. Accessed via the Internet at www.house.gov/ reform/hearings/healthcare/00.04.06/boyle. (Emphasis mine.)

9. Opening statement, Chairman Dan Burton, Government Reform Committee, U.S. House of Representatives, "Autism: Present Challenges, Future Needs—Why the Increased Rates?"; Thursday, April 6, 2000. Accessed 8/22/01 via the Internet at www.house.gov/reform/hear-ings/healthcare/00.04.06/opening_statement. (Emphasis mine.)

10. Merriam-Webster's Collegiate Dictionary, 10th Edition (Springfield, MA: 1994), s.v. "autism."

11. This information provided by the Autism-PDD (Pervasive Development Disorder) Network. Accessed on 8-21-2001 via the Internet at www.autism-pdd.net. (Emphasis mine.)

12. See Ben F. Feingold, M.D., Why Your Child Is Hyperactive (New York: Random House, 1974); and William G. Crook, M.D., and Laura Stevens, Solving the Puzzle of Your Hard-to-Raise Child (New York: Random House, 1987). Although these books focus primarily on ADD and ADHD, the information provided also applies to autism as many children with autism spectrum disorders also exhibit symptoms of ADD or ADHD.

13. Megson, "Is Autism a G-Alpha Protein Defect Reversible With Natural Vitamin A?", accessed through the Autism Research Institute on 8/21/01 via the Internet at www.autism.com/ari/megson. This article was presented publicly at the 1999 Defeat Autism Now! (DAN!) conference.

14. Mendelsohn, Confessions of a Medical Heretic, 132.

15. UNICEF Report: "The State of the World's Children

1998: Focus on Nutrition," Figure 11, "Measles deaths and vitamin A supplementation," accessed 2/29/01 via the Internet at www.unicef.org/sowc98. Figure 11 in the report specifically cites Alfred Sommer and Keith P. West, Jr., *Vitamin A Deficiency: Health, survival and vision* (New York and Oxford, England: Oxford University Press, 1996), 41, 48, 66–70.

16. Megson, "Is Autism a G-Alpha Protein Defect Reversible With Natural Vitamin A?"

17. Ibid.

18. This information provided by the Autism-PDD (Pervasive Development Disorder) Network. Accessed on 8-21-2001 via the Internet at www.autism-pdd.net.

19. Ibid.

20. India Abroad News Service, "Autistic boy's literary prowess storms Britain," December 13, 1999. Accessed via the Internet 8/28/01 at www.indianinfo.com.

Chapter 8
America's Love Affair With Mass Immunizations

1. CBS News correspondent Bob Orr, "For Some, Horrible Side Effects," CBS News, September 9, 2000. Accessed via the Internet at www.cbsnews.com/now/story/0,1597,231995-412,00.shtml.

2. Mendelsohn, *How to Raise a Healthy Child...in Spite of Your Doctor*, 232. Note: All of the items on this list appear in Dr. Mendelsohn's writings with the exception of autistic spectrum disorders and ADHD. These two items were included based on more recent research amply cited in this book.

3. Ibid., 233.

4. UNICEF: The State of the World's Children 1998: Focus on Nutrition: "Bringing Science to Bear." "...In three separate trials of children hospitalized with measles—one as early as 1932—deaths among children given high-dose vitamin A supplements were significantly lower than among children not supplemented.

The consistent results suggest that *a change in vitamin A status can rapidly alter basic physiological functions concerned with cellular repair and resistance to infection, thereby saving lives.*" (Alfred Sommer and Keith P. West, Jr., *Vitamin A Deficiency: Health, survival and vision* [New York and Oxford: Oxford University Press, 1996], 41, 48, 66–70). Accessed via the Internet at www.unicef.org/sowc98.

5. Ibid. "…Two other treatments during pregnancy are also under investigation. These involve either intravenous therapy with purified anti-HIV antibodies, or supplementation with vitamin A. In a 1994 study of HIV-infected women in Malawi, it was found that 32 percent of those who were vitamin A deficient during pregnancy had passed HIV on to their infants. In contrast, only 7 percent of HIV-infected women with sufficient levels of vitamin A did so. The study concluded that vitamin A-deficient women were thus four and a half times more likely to infect their children." (Richard D. Semba, "Will vitamin A supplementation reduce mother-to-child transmission of HIV?", *Research in Action*, No. 5, UNICEF, New York, July 1996). "Also, a 1995 study from Kenya reported that the concentration of HIV in breast milk is higher in vitamin A-deficient mothers than in those with good vitamin A status. Another study, also from Kenya, has shown that HIV-positive women who are also vitamin A deficient were five times more likely than non-vitamin A-deficient women to shed HIV-infected cells in their reproductive tracts, a factor that may be an important determinant of both sexual and vertical transmission of AIDS. However, some experts have suggested that these results may have come about not because of the influence of vitamin A on HIV transmission, but because poor vitamin A status and high rates of infection occur together for other reasons. Based on the findings of the first studies—and to demonstrate whether the connection between vitamin A and HIV transmission is causal—four clinical trials were begun recently to examine HIV transmission rates in women who have received vitamin A supplements during the second or third trimester of pregnancy. Results from these studies, conducted in Malawi, South

Africa, Tanzania and Zimbabwe on a total of nearly 3,000 HIV-infected women, are expected soon."

6. "Vaccine Refusal May Cause NY to Take Children," *Healthkeepers* (Spring–Summer 2001): 10.

7. Ibid.

8. Ibid.

9. James Murphy, *What Every Parent Should Know About Childhood Immunization* (Boston: Earth Healing Products, 1998), 63, citing Louis Dublin and Alfred Lotka, *Twenty-Five Years of Health Progress* (New York: Metropolitan Life Insurance Company, 1937), 48.

10. Ibid., 45.

11. Ibid., citing Louis Dublin, *Health Progress 1936-1945* (New York: Metropolitan Life Insurance Company, 1948), 12.

12. Mendelsohn, *How to Raise a Healthy Child...in Spite of Your Doctor*, 236–237.

13. N. Halsey et al., "Risk Factors in Subacute Sclerosing Panencephalitis," *Am. J. Epidemiology* 111 (1980): 415–424.

14. Murphy, *What Every Parent Should Know About Childhood Immunization*, 111, citing CDC unpublished data. *MMWR* 1990;39(19):326.

15. Ibid., 112, Table 11-1: "14 Investigated Outbreaks of Measles in 1977," Immunization Division, Bureau of State Services, and Field Service Division, Bureau of Epidemiology, Centers for Disease Control. *MMWR* 1977;26(14):109.

16. Neil Z. Miller, *Vaccines: Are They Really Safe and Effective?* (Sante Fe, NM: New Atlantean Press, 1998), 25, citing *National Health Federation Bulletin* (November 1969).

17. Ibid., 26, citing *FDA Workshop to Review Warnings, Use Instructions, and Precautionary Information [on Vaccines]* (Rockland, MD: September 18, 1992), 27.

18. Murphy, *What Every Parent Should Know About Childhood Immunization*, 108–109, citing respectively MMWR 1990; 39(41):727–28 and H.F. Hull et al., "Risk Factors

for Measles Vaccine Failure Among Immunized Students," *Pediatrics* 76 (1985): 518–23.

19. Vijendra K. Singh, Ph.D., Department of Biology & Biotechnology Center, Utah State University, Logan, Utah; testifying before the Government Reform Committee, U.S. House of Representatives, April 6, 2000.

20. Mendelsohn, *How to Raise a Healthy Child...In Spite of Your Doctor*, 239.

21. Miller, *Vaccines: Are They Really Safe and Effective?*, 30, citing Dr. Allen B. Allen, "Is RA27/3 a Cause of Chronic Fatigue?" *Medical Hypothesis* 27 (1988): 217–220; and Dr. A. D. Lieberman, "The Role of the Rubella Virus in the Chronic Fatigue Syndrome," *Clinical Ecology*, Vol. 7, No. 3: 51–54.

22. Ibid., citing "Rubella Vaccine and Susceptible Hospital Employees: Poor Physician Participation," *Journal of the American Medical Association* (February 20, 1981).

23. Ibid., 24, citing November 20–21, 1975, Minutes of the 15th meeting of the Panel of Review of Bacterial Vaccines and Toxoids with Standards and Potency (presented by the Bureau of Biologics and the Food and Drug Administration).

24. Murphy, *What Every Parent Should Know About Childhood Immunization*, 87–91, lists the adverse reactions to the pertussis vaccine in its various forms and cites twenty-seven different scientific studies spanning an eighty-five-year period (many of them were conducted by agencies of the Federal government).

25. Ibid., 83, citing R.M. Barkin and M.E. Pichichero, "Diphtheria-Pertussis-Tetanus Vaccine: Reactogenicity of Commercial Products," *Pediatrics* 63, no. 2 (1979): 256–60.

26. Harris L. Coulter, Ph.D., and Barbara Loe Fisher, *A Shot in the Dark: Why the P in the DPT May Be Hazardous to Your Child's Health* (Garden City Park, NY: Avery Publishing Group, Inc., 1991), 74–75. This was one of the original "warning books" sounding the alarm about the dangers of the original DPT vaccine. Since then, the medical community has reluctantly admitted there were

problems with the vaccine and an allegedly "safer" pertussis vaccine was developed and inserted in the multiple-disease vaccine. Authors cite respectively C.A. Hannik, 1969. Major reactions after DPT-polio vaccination in the Netherlands. *International Symposium on Pertussis*, Bilthoven. *Symposium Series on Immunological Standardization* 13: 161–70. Basel, Munchen, New York: Karger; and J.M. Hopper, 1961. Illness after whooping cough vaccination. *Medical Officer* (October 20), 241–44.

27. Immunization Division, Bureau of State Services, and Field Services Division, Bureau of Epidemiology, Centers for Disease Control. *MMWR* 1977;26(14):109.

28. Coulter and Fisher, *A Shot in the Dark*, 72 (emphasis mine).

29. This research finding was discussed in detail in chapter 7, which cites Mary N. Megson, M.D., F.A.A.P., "Is Autism a G-Alpha Protein Defect Reversible With Natural Vitamin A?", a research article accessed through the Autism Research Institute on 8/21/01 at www.autism.com/ari/megson. This article was presented publicly at the 1999 Defeat Autism Now! (DAN!) conference.

30. Murphy, *What Every Parent Should Know About Childhood Immunization*, 76, citing John Taranger, "Mild Clinical Course of Pertussis in Swedish Infants of Today," *Lancet* (June 12, 1982): 1360, and Coulter and Fisher, *A Shot in the Dark* (New York: Harcourt Brace Jovanovich, 1985), 172 (an earlier edition than the one used in this book).

31. Ibid., p. 75, citing Paul Fine and Jacqueline Clarkson, "The Recurrence of Whooping Cough: Possible Implications for Assessment of Vaccine Efficacy," *Lancet* (March 20, 1982): 667.

32. Coulter and Fisher, *A Shot in the Dark*, 217.

33. Ibid., 212.

34. Miller, *Vaccines: Are They Really Safe and Effective?*, 32.

35. Ibid., 18–21, citing Michael Anderson, *International Mortality Statistics* (Washington, DC: Facts on File, 1981), 177–178.

36. *The Washington Post*, September 24, 1976.

37. 20th Immunization Conference Proceedings, Dallas, Texas, May 6–9, 1985, (U.S. Department of Health and Human Services, October 1985), 85.

38. Using a "polymerase chain reaction technique," the researchers identified SV40 DNA in archival tissue samples from the thirteen antibody-positive children for whom tissue samples were available. The researchers discovered SV40 DNA in tissue samples from four children: three kidney transplant patients and one patient with Wilms' tumor. A sample from one of the kidney transplant patients also yielded human polyomavirus BK virus DNA products. Sequence analysis showed that the SV40 DNA strains did not arise from laboratory contamination, the team reports. (*J Infect Disease* 180 [September 1999]: 884–887.)

39. Leon Chaitow, *Vaccination and Immunisation: Dangers, Delusions and Alternatives* (Saffron Walden, Essex [GB]: The C.W. Daniel Company Limited, 1998), 141.

40. Coulter and Fisher, *A Shot in the Dark*, 215.

41. Ibid., 204.

42. Ibid., 185.

43. Ibid., 219.

Chapter 9
Heavy Metals and Toxic Injections

1. Comments of Bernard Rimland, Ph.D., Director of Autism Research Institute (ARI), excerpted from the "Background and Introduction to the Position Paper of the Consensus Conference on the Mercury Detoxification of Autistic Children," released May 2001 by the Autism Research Institute and sponsored by "Defeat Autism Now! (DAN!) and supported in part by Kirkman Laboratories.

2. Jack Challem, "Gut feelings and the origins of autism," *Let's Live Magazine* (May 2001): 48.

3. "Position Paper of the Consensus Conference on the Mercury Detoxification of Autistic Children," released

May 2001 by the Autism Research Institute and sponsored by "Defeat Autism Now! (DAN!) and supported in part by Kirkman Laboratories.

4. Challem, "Gut feelings and the origins of autism," 46 (emphasis mine).

5. Ibid., 48.

6. "Top 20 Hazardous Substances ATSDR/EPA Priority List for 1999," published jointly and updated annually by the Agency for Toxic Substances and Disease Registry of the Centers for Disease Control (U.S. Department of Health and Human Services) and the Environmental Protection Agency. The ATSDR Information Center updated this information page on June 29, 2001. Accessed on 9/12/01 via the Internet at www.atsdr.cdc.gov/cxcx3.

7. Murphy, *What Every Parent Should Know About Childhood Immunization*, 53.

8. "ToxFAQs for Formaldehyde," CAS# 50-00-0, July 1999, Agency for Toxic Substances and Disease Registry, Division of Toxicology, Centers for Disease Control, U.S. Department of Health and Human Services, Public Health Service. The ATSDR Information Center updated this information page on June 29, 2001. Accessed on 9/12/01 via the Internet at www.atsdr.cdc.gov/toxfaq.

9. William G. Crook, M.D. and Laura J. Stevens, *Solving the Puzzle of Your Hard-to-Raise Child* (New York: Random House, Inc., 1987), 35.

10. Ben F. Feingold, M.D., *Why Your Child Is Hyperactive* (New York: Random House, 1975), 161 (emphasis mine).

11. Murphy, *What Every Parent Should Know About Childhood Immunization*, 55.

12. Ibid., 53, citing *Casarett and Doull's Toxicology, The Basic Science of Poisons*, 3rd. ed., Curtis Klaassen, Mary Amdur, John Doull, eds., (New York: MacMillan Publishing Company, 1986), 819.

13. Ibid., citing Robert Gosselin, Roger Smith, and Harold

Hodge, *Clinical Toxicology of Commercial Products*, 5th ed. (Baltimore, MD: Williams and Wilkins, 1984), sec. III-196.

14. Ibid., 55.

15. Ibid., 56–57, citing Marcus Mason, C.C. Cate, and John Baker, "Toxicology and Carcinogenesis of Various Chemicals Used in the Preparation of Vaccines," *Clinical Toxicology* 4 (1971): 185, 197, 200.

16. Chaitow, *Vaccination and Immunisation: Dangers, Delusions and Alternatives*, 62.

17. Feingold, *Why Your Child Is Hyperactive*, 163–164.

18. Ibid., 137 (emphasis mine).

19. See Crook, *Solving the Puzzle of Your Hard-to-Raise Child*, Chapter 26, "Overcoming Yeast-Connected Illness…Questions and Answers," 143–153.

20. Summarized excerpts drawn from the "Defeat Autism Now! (DAN!) Mercury Detoxification Consensus Group Position Paper," May 2001, Autism Research Institute, 4182 Adams Avenue, San Diego, California 92116. Autistic children, in particular, may benefit from the "DAN! Treatment Protocol," a systematic treatment designed through the work of the "Defeat Autism Now!" nonprofit organization. The DAN! Protocol is designed to safely restore proper balance to the digestive systems of children who exhibit deficient digestive system function.

Chapter 10
Reversing the Dietary Devastation
of the Television Generation

1. Lori G. Borrud, with co-authors Sharon Mickle, Alvin Nowverl and Katherine Tippett, "Eating Out in America: Impact on Food Choices and Nutrient Profiles" or "1994–1996 Continuing Survey of Food Intakes by Individuals" (CSFII), Food Surveys Research Group (FSRG), Beltsville Human Nutrition Research Center, Agricultural Research Center, U.S. Department of Agriculture, from material presented by Lori Borrud in a speech at the 124th Annual Meeting of the American

Public Health Association, November 20, 1996 (emphasis mine). Accessed via the Internet on 6/18/01 at www.barc.usda.gov/bhnrc/foodsurvey/Eatout95.

2. Ted and Sharon Broer, "Infant and Toddler Nutrition," an audiotape offering detailed information, suggested food choices and menus and nutritional supplements for optimal child nutrition. Call my office at (800) 726-1834 to order this audiotape.

3. Jamie Murphy, *What Every Parent Should Know About Childhood Immunization* (Boston, MA: Earth Healing Products, 1998), citing Arnold Goldman and C. Wayne Smith, "Host Resistance Factors in Human Milk," *Journal of Pediatrics* 82, no. 6 (1973): 1083.

4. Ibid., citing Albert Sabin and Howard Fieldsteel, "Antipoliomyelitic Activity of Human and Bovine Colostrum and Milk," *Journal of Pediatrics* 29 (1962): 115.

5. Sharon Broer, *Train Up Your Children in the Way They Should Eat* (Lake Mary, FL: Siloam Press, 1999), 116–121. Used by permission. This book and a complete cookbook filled with healthy and tasty menu options for parents who care about maximum family nutrition may be ordered through my office at Broer & Associates, (800) 726-1834.

6. The story of "Robbie" and the discussion of Dr. Feingold that follows were adapted from a copyrighted publication available through my office: Ted Broer, Ph.D., "Attention Deficit Disorder," *Eat, Drink & Be Healthy Report*, Vol. 1, No. 1 (1995): 7–12. You may order this detailed health report through my office at Broer & Associates, (800) 726-1834.

7. Ibid. This detailed nutritional report cites an extensive number of scientific studies related to the topic of food dyes and additives.

8. R. J. Prinz, et al., *J Behav. Ecology*, Vol 2, No.1 (1981).

9. L. Langseth and J. Dowd. "Glucose Tolerance and Hyperkinesis," *Food Cosmet. Toxico._16 (1978):129.

10. J. Egger, C Carter, P. Graham, D. Gumley and J. Soothill, "Controlled Trial of Oligoantigenic Treatment

in the Hyperkinetic Syndrome," *Lancet* (1985): 540–545.

11. P. Silva, C. Kirkland, A. Simpson, L. Stewart and S. Williams, "Some Developmental and Behavioral Problems with Bilateral Otitis Media with Effusion," *J Learning Disabil.* 15 (1982): 417–421; J. Reichman and W. Healey: "Learning Disabilities and Conductive Hearing Loss Involving Otitis Media," *J Learning Disabil.* 16 (1983): 272–278.

12. B. Worthington-Roberts, "Suboptimal Nutrition and Behavior in Children," Chapter 19 in *Contemporary Developments in Nutrition* (St. Louis, MO: C.V. Mosby, 1981), 55–62.

13. Brenner. "The Effects of Megadoses of Selected B-complex Vitamins on Children with Hyperkinesis: Controlled Studies with Long-term Follow Up," *J Learning Disabil.* 15 (1982): 258.

14. Hoffer. "Vitamin B_3-Dependent Child." *Schizophrenia* 3 (1971): 107–113.

15. Ted Broer, *Maximum Energy: Top Ten Foods Never to Eat, Top Ten Health Strategies to Feel Great* (Lake Mary, FL: Siloam Press, 1999).

Chapter 11
Keys to Proper Parental Control:
Consistency, Caring and Compassion

1. Videotape of "Crisis in the Classroom," a television Special Report hosted by Phyllis Schafly and produced by Eagle Forum, 1996.

2. Gary and Ann Marie Ezzo, *Growing Kids God's Way: Biblical Ethics for Parenting* (Simi Valley, CA: Growing Families International, 1999), 173. You may order this publication and many other excellent parenting tools from Growing Families International (800) 396-4434 or through their website at www.gfi.org.

3. Ibid., 174.

4. James Dobson, *The Strong-Willed Child* (Wheaton, IL: Living Books, a registered trademark of Tyndale House Publishing, Inc., 1985), 7, 11.

5. You may wish to contact the Autism Society of America Foundation via the Internet at www.autism-society.org; the Autism Research Institute, 4182 Adams Ave., San Diego, CA 92116; or the Sacramento-based Families for Early Autism Treatment (FEAT) via the Internet at www.feat.org. Some of the autism intervention programs in use include the following: "Treatment and Education of Autistic and related Communication handicapped Children (TEACCH)," developed by the University of North Carolina (Division TEACCH Administration and Research, CB# 7180, 310 Medical School Wing E, The University of North Carolina at Chapel Hill, Chapel Hill, North Carolina 27599-7180; 919-966-2174). "The Lovaas Institute for Early Intervention (LIFE)," a research-based institute that specializes in teaching preschool-age children with autism, pervasive developmental disorders and related developmental disabilities (LIFE, 11500 West Olympic Blvd, Ste 460, Los Angeles, CA 90064; 310-914-5433). "Floortime: A Treatment for Autistic Spectrum Disorders" developed by Stanley I. Greenspan, M.D., a Clinical Professor of Psychiatry, Behavioral Sciences and Pediatrics at the George Washington University Medical School. Contact The Interdisciplinary Council on Developmental and Learning Disorders (ICDLD), 4938 Hampden Lane, Suite 800, Bethesda, MD 20814, to order a twenty-hour training tape on the "DIR Model and Floor Time."

6. Dobson, *The Strong-Willed Child*, 13–14.

7. William J. Bennett, ed., *The Book of Virtues: A Treasury of Great Moral Stories* (New York: Simon & Schuster, 1993), 11.

8. Again, I don't condone child abuse in any form. Yet there is a clear distinction between the use of restrained and carefully applied corporal punishment and the "beating" of a child in anger using the hand, foot or any other instrument. When I was in elementary school, junior high school and high school, it was common throughout the United States for school authorities to administer "pops on the bottom" to students who refused verbal

warnings and ignored progressively more serious punishments. In my case, I remember receiving correction administered with big, wide redwood paddles when we failed to listen to correction. It never "damaged" my friends or me, but it *did* capture our attention and modify our behavior with uncommon effectiveness.

Chapter 12
Survival Strategies for Caring Parents

1. I encourage you to get more information and practical tips about fasting by obtaining a copy of our *Eat, Drink & Be Healthy!* program. These publications are available through my office at (800) 726-1834.

2. Be aware that many if not most medical doctors wholeheartedly endorse childhood vaccinations, but very few have conducted objective research since their days in medical school. Consult with your doctor, but reserve for yourself the right to make all medical decisions for your child. You are likely to experience great pressure at the hospital or clinic to allow your child to receive multiple injections even before they leave the maternity unit. The only way you can hope to preserve your right of choice is to do your research and make your decisions about the routine vaccination of your newborn *ahead of time*.

3. Broer, *Maximum Energy*, 15, citing "Dietary Goals for the United States," Washington, DC: Government Printing Office, stock no. 052-070-03913-2.

**If you enjoyed Maximum Solutions for ADD,
Learning Disabilities and Autism,** *here are some other*
titles from Siloam Press that we think will help you
live in health—body, mind and spirit...

Maximum Energy
Ted Broer
ISBN: 0-88419-643-7
Retail Price: $19.99

Would you like to see a significant improvement in your energy
levels and general health in only thirty days—no matter how you
currently feel? Ted Broer will show you how and why it can happen in your life if you begin to make wise dietary and exercise
choices today. Right choices will quickly give you the maximum
energy you need to double your energy in just thirty days!

Train Up Your Children in the Way They Should Eat
Sharon Broer
ISBN: 0-88419-663-1
Retail Price: $13.99

We're raising a generation of children at risk. But you can
shield your children from painful ear infections, miserable allergies, life-threatening asthma, obesity, poor health and even
death—if you're willing to make simple changes right now in
your family diet. Step by step, learn how to reap the guaranteed
rewards of good nutrition.

A Healthy Heart
Francisco Contreras, M.D.
ISBN: 0-88419-765-4
Retail Price: $19.99

Even if you've never experienced heart problems, you need to read
this book. In it noted oncologist Dr. Francisco Contreras shares his
medical expertise and wisdom as he explains the causes and treatments
for heart disease. You will learn why technology can't always help, and
you'll discover powerful keys for reclaiming heart health.

Living in Health—Body, Mind and Spirit

To pick up a copy of any of these titles, contact
your local Christian bookstore or order online
at www.charismawarehouse.com.